Oregon Legal Research

Oregon Legal Research

Suzanne E. Rowe

CAROLINA ACADEMIC PRESS
Durham, North Carolina

ISBN 0-89089-539-2
LCCN 2003110323

Carolina Academic Press
700 Kent Street
Durham, NC 27701
Telephone (919) 489-7486
Fax (919) 493-5668
www.cap-press.com

Printed in the United States of America

Summary of Contents

Contents

Preface

The primary audience for this book includes first-year law students who are enrolled in a course that integrates hands-on research with legal analysis and writing. Other audiences include practitioners who need to become familiar with Oregon resources as well as paralegals, college students, and even laypeople.

I began writing concise, state-specific research books when my students objected to the lengthy, nationally renowned texts that I had assigned. While librarians and professors — myself included — value those texts for their breadth of coverage and their detailed explanations of minute points, the students found them overwhelming and confusing. The students wanted to read just enough to enable them to learn actively by locating and viewing the resources themselves in the library or online. They also wanted to know how to conduct research specifically for the state where they were attending law school, would likely find their first legal jobs, and may spend their entire professional careers.

My initial response to their concerns was *Florida Legal Research: Sources, Process, and Analysis.*[1] This book is my second response, attempting to provide Oregon law students and other legal researchers with an accessible, but meaningful introduction to legal research in this state.

---

1. Suzanne E. Rowe, Barbara J. Busharis, & Lisa Kuhlman Tietig, *Florida Legal Research: Sources, Process, & Analysis* (Carolina Academic Press 1998); Barbara J. Busharis & Suzanne E. Rowe, *Florida Legal Research: Sources, Process, & Analysis* (2d ed., Carolina Academic Press 2002).

I have tried to keep the book as short as possible (remembering that students may not read lengthier research texts) while recognizing the varying backgrounds of those who might use the book. Excerpts of sample pages[2] are included only when law students might need them for context before going to the library. Discussion of legal analysis is included as a crucial element in legal research, but that discussion is limited since the book's main focus is the *process* of performing research. The researcher who understands the process of legal research can transfer this skill from one research project to another, from state to federal resources, and from print sources to online materials.

On the few occasions that students require more detailed information, usually for federal research sources, I gladly refer them to the texts listed in Appendix B. Also in that appendix are texts on legal writing and analysis, as well as bibliographic sources on Oregon research.

Suzanne E. Rowe
June 2003

---

2. In some instances, the format of these excerpts has been adapted to fit the small page size of this book.

Acknowledgments

A large number of people have contributed to this small volume. For review of complete drafts at various stages of the project, I am extremely grateful to Dennis Hyatt, Sam Jacobson, Steve Johansen, Joan Malmud, Angus Nesbit, Amy Sloan, and Kyu Ho Youm. Additionally, David Olsson and David Schuman reviewed chapters in areas of law where I had the least experience and most needed support. I appreciate the insights and suggestions each of you offered.

Numerous colleagues at the University of Oregon School of Law reviewed portions of the manuscript or discussed their areas of expertise with me. Naming each of them would merely boast the collegiality that exists at the law school. I have to note particularly, though, the librarians at the John E. Jaqua Law Library, who have been invaluable from the moment I arrived in Eugene three years ago. They taught me their secrets, tracked down elusive answers, and reviewed drafts of the manuscript. Many thanks go to Dennis Hyatt, Mary Clayton, Stephanie Midkiff, and Angus Nesbit. Special thanks are also due to Donna Williamson, the Legal Research and Writing Program Assistant, for her constant support.

I am indebted to my co-authors of *Florida Legal Research*, Barbara J. Busharis and Lisa Kuhlman Tietig. While this book is a new work, I undoubtedly included ideas from our earlier collaboration. I also acknowledge the contributions of authors of other research texts, especially those in Appendix B.

I have been blessed with outstanding research assistants. Greena Ng worked with me for two years, and her imprint appears on every page (except this one). Jennifer Hisey, Marcus Reed, and Tim Hering provided exceptional research and editing assistance.

Students at Oregon for the past three years have used draft chapters of this book in Legal Research and Writing classes, and many students offered comments that improved the final product. I am indebted especially to the students in Section G for their critiques and their support. Learning from students is one of the greatest joys of teaching.

I am grateful for the support of the University of Oregon's Office of Research and Faculty Development, which provided me with a New Faculty Award. I also acknowledge the generous support of the Love, Moore, Banks and Grebe Endowment Fund.

My greatest thanks go to Mark Corley for reminding me daily that life exists outside the law school, too.

SER

Oregon Legal Research

Chapter 1

The Research Process and Legal Analysis

I. Oregon Legal Research

The fundamentals of legal research are the same in every American jurisdiction, though the details vary. While some variations are minor, others require specialized knowledge of the resources available and the analytical framework in which those resources are used. This book focuses on the resources and analysis required to be thorough and effective in researching Oregon law. It supplements this focus with brief explanations of federal research and research into the law of other states, both to introduce other resources and to highlight some of the variations.

II. The Intersection of Legal Research and Legal Analysis

Most students realize in the first week of law school that legal analysis is difficult. At the same time, some consider legal research simplistic busy work. The basic process of legal research *is* simple. For most print resources, you will begin with an index, find entries that appear relevant, read those sections of the text, and then find out whether more recent information is available. For most online research, you will search particular websites or databases using words likely to appear in the text of relevant documents.

Legal analysis is interwoven throughout this process, raising challenging questions. In print research, which words will you look up in the index? How will you decide whether an index entry looks promising? With online research, how will you choose relevant words and construct a search most likely to produce the documents you need? When you read the text of a document, how will you determine whether it is relevant to your client's situation? How will you learn whether more recent material changed the law or merely applied it in a new situation? The answer to each of these questions requires legal analysis. This intersection of research and analysis can make legal research very difficult, especially for the novice. While this book's focus is legal research, it also includes the fundamental aspects of legal analysis required to conduct research competently.

This book is not designed to be a blueprint of every resource in the law library or search engine on the Internet; many resources contain their own detailed explanations in a preface or a "help" section. This book is more like a manual or field guide, introducing the resources needed at each step of the research process and explaining how to use them.

III. Types of Legal Authority

Before researching the law, you must be clear about the goal of your search. In every research situation, you will want to find constitutional provisions, statutes, administrative rules, and judicial opinions that control your client's situation. In other words, you are searching for primary, mandatory authority.

Law is often divided along two lines. The first line distinguishes primary authority from secondary authority. *Primary authority* is law produced by government bodies with law-making power. Legislatures write statutes; courts write judicial opinions; and administrative agencies write rules (also called regulations). *Secondary authority* includes all other legal sources, such as treatises, law review articles, and legal encyclopedias. These secondary sources are designed to aid you in understanding the law and locating primary authority.

Another division is made between mandatory and persuasive authority. *Mandatory authority* is binding on the court that would decide a conflict if the situation were litigated. In a question of Oregon law, mandatory or binding authority includes Oregon's constitution, statutes enacted by the Oregon legislature, opinions of the Supreme Court of Oregon,[1] and Oregon administrative rules. *Persuasive authority* is not binding, but may be followed if relevant and well reasoned. Authority may be merely persuasive if it is from a different jurisdiction or if it is not produced by a law-making body. In a question of Oregon law, examples of persuasive authority would include a similar California statute, an opinion of a Washington state court, and a law review article. Notice in Table 1-1 that persuasive authority may be either primary or secondary authority, while mandatory authority is always primary.

Table 1-1. Examples of Authority in Oregon Research

	Mandatory Authority	Persuasive Authority
Primary Authority	Oregon statutes Oregon Supreme Court cases	California statutes Washington Supreme Court cases
Secondary Authority	—	Law review articles Legal encyclopedias

Within primary, mandatory authority, there is an interlocking hierarchy of law involving constitutions, statutes, administrative rules, and judicial opinions. The constitution of each state is the supreme law of that state. If a statute is on point, that statute comes next in the hierarchy, followed by administrative rules. Judicial opinions may interpret the statute or rule, but they cannot disregard them. A judi-

---

1. An opinion from the Court of Appeals is binding on the trial courts if the Supreme Court of Oregon has not addressed a particular topic.

cial opinion may, however, decide that a statute violates the constitution or that a rule oversteps its bounds. If there is no constitutional
provision, statute, or administrative rule on point, the issue will be
controlled by *common law* or judge-made law.

IV. Court Systems

Because much legal research includes reading judicial opinions, researchers need to understand the court system. The basic court structure includes a trial court, an intermediate court of appeals, and an
ultimate appellate court, often called the "supreme" court.[2] These
courts exist at both the state and federal levels.

A. Oregon Courts

In Oregon, the trial courts are called circuit courts.[3] These courts
exist in each of Oregon's thirty-six counties.[4] Oregon's intermediate
court is called the Court of Appeals.[5] Located in Salem, the Court of
Appeals is composed of ten judges, who sit in three-judge panels, with
the Chief Judge acting as a substitute when needed. The Supreme
Court of Oregon, which also sits primarily in Salem, has seven justices.[6]
The seven justices sit *en banc* to hear all cases, unless a justice is recused.

---

2. The following description omits for brevity local courts and tribal
courts. Information on these courts is available on the state's website at www.
oregon.gov, under the "Government" link.

3. In addition to the circuit courts, since 1961, the Oregon Tax Court has
served as the trial court for all cases in which Oregon tax law is at issue. Appeals from decisions of this court go to the Oregon Supreme Court, not the
Court of Appeals.

4. The state is divided into twenty-seven judicial districts; each district
includes one to five counties.

5. Prior to 1969, Oregon's judicial system consisted of two tiers: trial
courts and the Oregon Supreme Court. In 1969, a three-tier system was created with the establishment of the intermediate Court of Appeals.

6. A jurist on the highest court is called a "justice" while on lower courts
the term "judge" is used.

The website for the Oregon judiciary is www.ojd.state.or.us. It contains a wealth of information, including a map of Oregon's circuit courts; links to courts maintaining websites; an explanation of the jurisdiction of state courts; lists of court personnel; and recent opinions of the appellate courts.

B. Federal Courts

In the federal judicial system, the trial courts are called United States District Courts. There are ninety-four district courts in the federal system, with each district drawn from a particular state. A state with a relatively small population may not be subdivided into smaller geographic regions. The entire state of Oregon, for example, makes up the federal District of Oregon. Even so, district courts are located in three cities: Portland, Eugene, and Medford. States with larger populations and higher caseloads are subdivided into more districts. For example, California has four federal districts: northern, central, southern, and eastern. Washington has two federal districts: eastern and western.

Intermediate appellate courts in the federal system are called United States Courts of Appeals. There are courts of appeals for each of the thirteen federal circuits. Twelve of these circuits are based on geographic jurisdiction. In addition to eleven numbered circuits covering all the states, there is the District of Columbia Circuit. The thirteenth federal circuit, called the Federal Circuit, hears appeals from district courts in all other circuits on issues related to patent law and from certain specialized courts and agencies. A map showing the federal circuits is available at www.uscourts.gov/links.html. Circuit maps may also be found in the front of the *Federal Supplement* and the *Federal Reporter*, books that publish the cases decided by federal courts.

Oregon is in the Ninth Circuit. This means that cases from the United States District Court for the District of Oregon are appealed to the United States Court of Appeals for the Ninth Circuit. This circuit encompasses Alaska, Arizona, California, Hawaii, Idaho, Montana, Nevada, Oregon, and Washington, as well as Guam and the Northern Mariana Islands.

The highest court in the federal system is the United States Supreme Court. It decides cases concerning the United States Constitution and federal statutes. This court does not have the final say on matters of purely state law; that authority rests with the highest court of each state. Parties who wish to have the U.S. Supreme Court hear their case must file a petition for *certiorari*, as the court has discretion over which cases it hears.

The website for the federal judiciary contains maps, court addresses, explanations of jurisdiction, and other helpful information. The address is www.uscourts.gov.

C. Courts of Other States

Not all states have the three-tier court system of Oregon and the federal judiciary. A number of states do not have an intermediate appellate court, just as Oregon did not until 1969. Another difference in some court systems is that the "supreme" court is not the highest court. In New York, the trial courts are called supreme courts and the highest court is the Court of Appeals. Two other states, Massachusetts and Maine, call their highest court the Supreme Judicial Court.

Citation manuals are good references for learning the names and hierarchy of the courts, as well as for learning proper citation to legal authorities. The two most popular are the *ALWD Citation Manual: A Professional System of Citation,* written by Dean Darby Dickerson and the Association of Legal Writing Directors,[7] and *The Bluebook: A Uniform System of Citation,* written by students from several law schools.[8] Appendix 1 of both manuals provides information on federal and state courts.

---

7. ALWD & Darby Dickerson, *ALWD Citation Manual* (2d ed., Aspen Publishers 2003) ("*ALWD Manual*"). Most citations in this book conform to the *ALWD Manual* unless there is a clear preference in Oregon for a different form.

8. *The Bluebook: A Uniform System of Citation* (The Columbia Law Review et al. eds., 17th ed., The Harvard Law Review Assn. 2000).

V. Overview of the Research Process

Conducting effective legal research means following a process. This process leads to the authority that controls a legal issue as well as to commentary that may help you analyze new and complex legal matters. The outline in Table 1-2 presents the basic research process.

Table 1-2. Overview of the Research Process

1. Generate a list of *research terms*.
2. Consult *secondary sources* and practice aids, including treatises, legal encyclopedias, and law review articles.
3. Find controlling *constitutional provisions*, *statutes*, or *rules* by reviewing their indexes for your research terms, then reading the relevant sections.
4. Use *digests* to find citations to cases. A digest is essentially a multi-volume topic index of cases in a certain jurisdiction or subject area.
5. Read the cases in *reporters*. A reporter series publishes the full text of cases in a certain jurisdiction or subject area.
6. *Update* or "Shepardize" your legal authorities to ensure they have not been repealed, reversed, modified, or otherwise changed.
7. *Outline* your legal analysis based on your research and *begin writing* your document.

This basic process should be customized for each research project. Consider whether you need to follow all seven steps, and if so, in what order. If you are unfamiliar with an area of law, you should follow each step of the process in the order indicated. Beginning with secondary sources will provide both context for the issues you must research and citations to relevant primary authority. As you gain experience in researching legal questions, you may choose to modify the process. For example, if you know that a situation is controlled by a statute, you may choose to begin with that step.

A. Generating Research Terms

Many legal resources in print use lengthy indexes as the starting point for finding legal authority. Electronic sources often require the researcher to enter words that are likely to appear in a synopsis or in the full text of relevant documents. To ensure you are thorough in beginning a research project, you will need a comprehensive list of words, terms, and phrases that may lead to law on point. These may be legal terms or common words that describe the client's situation. The items on this list are *research terms*.

Organized brainstorming is the best way to compile a comprehensive list of research terms. Some researchers ask the journalistic questions: Who? What? How? Why? When? Where? Others use a mnemonic device like TARPP, which stands for Things, Actions, Remedies, People, and Places.[9] Whether you use one of these suggestions or develop your own method, generate a broad range of research terms regarding the facts, issues, and desired solutions of your client's situation. Include in the list both specific and general words. Try to think of synonyms and antonyms for each term since at this point you are uncertain which terms an index may include. Using a legal dictionary or thesaurus may generate additional terms.

Table 1-3. Generating Research Terms
Journalistic Approach

Who:	Thief, robber, burglar, business owner, property owner
What:	Burglary, first degree, second degree, crime
How:	Breaking and entering, burglar tools, trespassing
Why:	Theft, stealing, stolen goods
When:	Midnight
Where:	Store, building, commercial establishment, business, shop

TARPP Approach

Things:	Burglar tool, stolen goods
Actions:	Burglary, breaking and entering, trespassing, damages, crime
Remedies:	First degree, second degree, incarceration
People:	Thief, robber, burglar, business owner, property owner
Places:	Store, building, commercial establishment, business, shop

---

9. *See* Roy M. Mersky & Donald J. Dunn, *Fundamentals of Legal Research* 15 (8th ed., Found. Press 2002) (explaining "TARP," a similar mnemonic device).

As an example, assume you are working for a defense attorney who was recently assigned to a burglary case. Around midnight, your client allegedly bent a credit card to spring the lock to a stereo store, where she stole $2,000 worth of equipment. She was charged with first-degree burglary. You have been asked to determine whether there is a good argument for limiting the charge to second-degree burglary based on the fact that she used a credit card and not professional burglar tools. Table 1-3 provides examples of research terms you might use to begin work on this project.

As your research progresses, you will learn new research terms to include in the list and decide to take others off. For example, you may read cases that give you insights into the key words judges tend to use in discussing this topic. Or you may learn a "term of art," a word or phrase that has special meaning in a particular area of law. These need to be added to the list.

B. Researching the Law—Organization of This Text

The remainder of this book explains how to use your research terms to conduct legal research in a variety of sources. Although the research process often begins with secondary sources, the book begins with primary authority because that authority is the goal of research. Chapter 2 addresses the Oregon Constitution, which is the highest legal authority in the state. Chapters 3 and 4 explain how to use reporters and digests to research judicial decisions. Chapters 5 and 6 describe statutory and legislative history research, respectively. Chapter 7 addresses administrative law. After this focus on primary authority, the following chapters explain how to update legal authority using *Shepard's Citations* (Chapter 8) and how to use secondary sources and practice aids (Chapter 9).

Although each chapter includes relevant website addresses for online research,[10] Chapter 10 specifically delves into the advantages and disadvantages of online research and provides basic information for

---

10. An updated list of current web addresses will be maintained at www.law.uoregon.edu/faculty/srowe.

conducting legal research online. There are several reasons for delaying this discussion of online sources. First, once a researcher understands the process of research and the relationship between research and analysis, moving between print and online resources is not difficult. In fact, many electronic products are based conceptually on the print versions of the same material. Next, while almost all researchers have access to free Internet sources, the legal resources available there are limited. Some offices, especially in public interest areas, still do not have wide access to commercial online products, so researchers in those settings must use books. Third, online products change so rapidly that a book with detailed information on the subject would soon become outdated. Finally, more senior attorneys may not be familiar with computerized research. For the foreseeable future, a junior attorney relying on electronic sources may need to convince a supervisor that the research was thorough; this may involve explaining the connection between print and electronic search methods.

Chapter 11 discusses research strategies as well as how to organize your research. You may prefer to skim that chapter now and refer to it frequently, even though a number of references in it will not become clear until you have read the intervening chapters.

Appendix A provides an overview of the conventions lawyers follow in citing legal authority in their documents. Appendix B contains a selected bibliography of texts on legal research and analysis. The general research texts tend to concentrate on federal resources, supplementing this book's brief introduction to those resources.

VI. Rules Governing Attorney Conduct

Conducting effective research is an important part of an attorney's role in assisting clients. The Oregon Code of Professional Responsibility[11] covers all aspects of legal practice. One part of the Code states

---

11. The Oregon Code of Professional Responsibility is available in a book entitled *Oregon Rules of Court: State.* The Code is available on the Oregon State Bar's website at www.osbar.org/2practice/rulesregs/cpr.htm.

"A lawyer shall provide competent representation to a client. Competent representation requires the legal knowledge, skill, thoroughness and preparation reasonably necessary for the representation."[12] A large part of this knowledge and preparation comes from legal research. This book provides instruction in how to conduct effective and efficient research into Oregon law.

---

12. Disciplinary Rule 6-101.

Chapter 2

The Oregon Constitution

"We the people of the State of Oregon
to the end that Justice be established,
order maintained, and liberty perpetuated,
do ordain this Constitution."[1]

The Oregon Constitution was written and approved by the people of the Oregon Territory in 1857. It became effective on February 14, 1859, when Oregon was admitted to the Union.[2]

The provisions of the Oregon Constitution parallel many of the most familiar provisions of the United States Constitution. Article I of Oregon's constitution ensures religious freedom, the right to a jury trial, and freedom from unreasonable search and seizure. Articles IV through VII provide for the legislative, executive, administrative, and judicial departments of the state government.

Like many state constitutions, the Oregon Constitution also covers some issues often thought of as being more statutory in nature. For example, in addition to the provisions mentioned above, Article I gives the state the power to permit the sale of liquor by the glass. Table 2-1 lists the articles of Oregon's constitution. Because of the breadth of issues covered by the Oregon Constitution, you should check to see whether a constitutional provision affects your research problem even when that possibility may seem unlikely.

---

1. *Preamble to the Oregon Constitution.*
2. For a fascinating introduction to these events, see David Schuman, *The Creation of the Oregon Constitution*, 74 Or. L. Rev. 611, 640 (1995).

Table 2-1. Articles of the Constitution of Oregon

Article I	Bill of Rights
Article II	Suffrage and Elections
Article III	Distribution of Powers
Article IV	Legislative Department
Article V	Executive Department
Article VI	Administrative Department
Article VII	(Amended) Judicial Department
Article VII	(Original) The Judicial Department
Article VIII	Education and School Lands
Article IX	Finance
Article X	The Militia
Article XI	Corporations and Internal Improvements
Article XI-A	Farm and Home Loans to Veterans
Article XI-D	State Power Development
Article XI-E	State Reforestation
Article XI-F(1)	Higher Education Building Projects
Article XI-F(2)	Veterans' Bonus
Article XI-G	Higher Education Institutions and Activities; Community Colleges
Article XI-H	Pollution Control
Article XI-I(1)	Water Development Projects
Article XI-I(2)	Multifamily Housing for Elderly and Disabled
Article XI-J	Small Scale Local Energy Loans
Article XI-K	Guarantee of Bonded Indebtedness of Educational Districts
Article XI-L	Oregon Health and Science University
Article XI-M	Seismic Rehabilitation of Public Education Buildings
Article XI-N	Seismic Rehabilitation of Emergency Services Buildings
Article XII	State Printing
Article XIV	Seat of Government
Article XV	Miscellaneous
Article XVI	Boundaries
Article XVII	Amendments and Revisions
Article XVIII	Schedule

I. Researching the Oregon Constitution

The Oregon Constitution is published in full every two years in *Oregon Revised Statutes* (ORS). Immediately following the Oregon Constitution, ORS provides an index specifically for the constitution. Currently, the constitution and its index are located in volume 15. ORS also contains a general index that provides references to the state constitution as well as to Oregon statutes.

As explained in Chapter 1, begin your research by generating a list of research terms from the facts and issues of your problem. Search the indexes for your terms and record the references given. For example, the general index contains under the term "Searches and Seizures" references both to Article I, Section 9 of the Oregon Constitution as well as to related statutes.

To find cases and other authorities that have discussed a certain provision of the state constitution, turn to the last volume of ORS, entitled "Annotations." These annotations are references to cases,[3] Attorney General Opinions,[4] and law review articles.[5] Each annotation contains a brief summary of the source referenced and its citation, which will enable you to locate the full source. You must not rely on the short summary; reading the text of the source itself will allow you to analyze its relevance to your research.

Annotations for constitutional provisions are listed near the end of the volume, after annotations for Oregon statutes. There is no table of contents for the annotations volume; simply skim through the volume until you see headings that refer to article and section numbers. Under the caption for the constitutional article and section that you are researching, you will find the annotations. If there are many annotations for that article and section, you may also find a short outline of annotations that appears just before the annotations them-

---

3. Chapter 3 explains how to find cases in reporters.

4. These opinions are explained in Chapter 7, Part IV.

5. The ORS annotations include unique abbreviations for the state's law reviews: OLR is *Oregon Law Review*, WLR is *Willamette Law Review*, and EL is *Environmental Law* (published by Lewis & Clark Law School). Law review articles are covered in Chapter 9, Part III.

Table 2-2. Excerpt of Annotations for Oregon Constitution

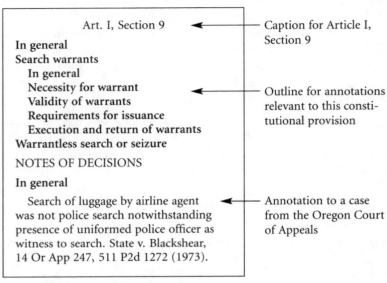

Art. I, Section 9 ◄——— Caption for Article I, Section 9

In general
Search warrants
  In general
  Necessity for warrant ◄——— Outline for annotations relevant to this constitutional provision
  Validity of warrants
  Requirements for issuance
  Execution and return of warrants
Warrantless search or seizure

NOTES OF DECISIONS

In general

  Search of luggage by airline agent ◄——— Annotation to a case from the Oregon Court of Appeals
was not police search notwithstanding
presence of uniformed police officer as
witness to search. State v. Blackshear,
14 Or App 247, 511 P2d 1272 (1973).

Source: *Oregon Revised Statutes*, volume 19, page 749 (2002 Supp.).

selves, as shown in Table 2-2. Otherwise, all the annotations for that section will be listed together.

The annotations volume of ORS is republished annually and includes annotations to authority since 1971. To find annotations to earlier authority, use the Compiled Annotations published as part of the 1971 edition of ORS. The annotations listed in these sources for each constitutional provision do not represent every authority that may be relevant to your research. Chapter 4 explains how to use *digests* to find additional cases on point, and Chapter 9 explains using *secondary sources* as research tools.

The full text of the constitution is available on the state's website at www.leg.state.or.us/orcons/home.html. This site contains the preamble and a search engine, too. Another site containing the text of the Oregon Constitution also has an index and a search engine for assistance in searching; the address is www.leg.state.or.us/billsset.htm.

Although ORS is available online at www.leg.state.or.us/ors, that site's organization does not strictly follow the print version. The ORS website does not include the text of the state constitution, even though the Annotations link references sections of the constitution.

II. Interpreting the Oregon Constitution

How a provision of the Oregon Constitution is interpreted by Oregon courts depends on whether the provision was part of the original constitution in 1859 or was added later by referral to the voters from the legislature or through the initiative process.

A. The *Priest* Framework

The Oregon Supreme Court has provided a framework for interpreting original provisions of the state's constitution. "There are three levels on which that constitutional provision must be addressed: Its specific wording, the case law surrounding it, and the historical circumstances that led to its creation."[6]

1. Text and Caselaw

Begin by reading the words of the constitutional provision carefully. If it is a lengthy provision, outlining it may help. Then read cases that address that provision. Also, reading the cases cited in those cases may provide important context.

Do not assume that cases interpreting the federal constitution also interpret Oregon's constitution. State constitutions can grant citizens *more* protection than is provided by the federal constitution, and Oregon's constitution does so. Even when the text of the Oregon Constitution is almost identical to the text of the United States Constitution, the Oregon Supreme Court may have interpreted it differently. For example, Article I, Section 9 of the Oregon Constitution contains almost the

---

6. *Priest v. Pearce*, 314 Or. 411, 415–16 (1992).

Table 2-3. Comparison of Constitutional Wording Regarding Unreasonable Search and Seizure

Oregon Constitution
Article I, Section 9

No law shall violate the right of the people to be secure in their persons, houses, papers, and effects, against unreasonable search, or seizure; and no warrant shall issue but upon probable cause, supported by oath, or affirmation, and particularly describing the place to be searched, and the person or thing to be seized.

United States Constitution
Fourth Amendment

The right of the people to be secure in their persons, houses, papers, and effects, against unreasonable searches and seizures, shall not be violated, and no Warrants shall issue, but upon probable cause, supported by Oath or affirmation, and particularly describing the place to be searched, and the persons or things to be seized.

---

same text as the Fourth Amendment to the United States Constitution (see Table 2-3), but Oregon's Supreme Court has interpreted the state constitution to provide more protection in this area than the federal constitution does.[7]

2. Historical Circumstances

For frugality reasons, the drafters of the Oregon Constitution decided against retaining an official reporter despite the significance of this historical event.[8] The *Journal of the Constitutional Convention* contains only a record of the official actions of the delegates, so it is of limited value. In 1926, long after the Oregon Constitution was adopted, Charles H. Carey collected the various newspaper accounts from the convention and combined them with entries from the *Journal*. The resulting book, *The Oregon Constitution and Proceedings and*

---

7. *E.g. State v. Caraher*, 293 Or. 741, 750–51 (1982); *State v. Tanner*, 304 Or. 312, 315 (1987).

8. David Schuman, *The Creation of the Oregon Constitution*, 74 Or. L. Rev. 611, 619 (1995).

Debates of the Constitutional Convention of 1857,[9] is an invaluable resource for understanding the historical circumstances surrounding Oregon's constitution and is cited frequently by courts.[10] Both the *Journal* and the Carey book, as well as other historical materials, are available on a microfiche set called *State Constitutional Conventions,* published by Congressional Information Service.

Until recently, *The Oregon Constitution and Proceedings* compilation was the primary source of information regarding the drafting of the state's constitution. However, a three-part series of articles by Professor Claudia Burton entitled *A Legislative History of the Oregon Constitution of 1857* now provides indispensable insights into the drafters' intent.[11] In a box of materials recently discovered at the Oregon Historical Society, Professor Burton found a nearly intact set of documents for each article of the Oregon Constitution. Her articles compile and comment on these documents. Reviewing the information in her articles is critical to understanding the historical background of the state constitution. As Judge David Schuman observed, "[A]ny attorney who writes a memorandum or brief... [on] the Oregon Constitution without first having consulted Professor Burton's article[s] is risking malpractice."[12]

In examining the historical circumstances of Oregon's constitution, Oregon courts look to other material as well. The Magna Carta and

---

9. *The Oregon Constitution and Proceedings and Debates of the Constitutional Convention of 1857* (Charles H. Carey ed., State Printing Dept. 1926).

10. Caution should be used when referencing the articles in this book, however, since major newspaper editors were also delegates at the convention. Schuman, *supra* n. 8, at 622.

11. Claudia Burton & Andrew Grade, *A Legislative History of the Oregon Constitution of 1857 - Part I (Articles I & II)*, 37 Willamette L. Rev. 469 (2001); Claudia Burton, *A Legislative History of the Oregon Constitution of 1857 (Frame of Government: Articles III–VII)*, 39 Willamette L. Rev. 245 (2003). The remainder of the Oregon Constitution will be covered in a third article.

12. David Schuman, Lecture, *Back to the Future, Forward to the Past: The Oregon Supreme Court's New History Fetish* (Univ. Or. Sch. Law Oct. 19, 2001) (CLE handout on file with author).

English legal commentators are sometimes cited. Realize, too, that the drafters modeled the Oregon Constitution after the Indiana Constitution's Bill of Rights. A chart by W.C. Palmer entitled *The Sources of the Oregon Constitution* compares sections of Oregon's constitution to the constitutions of Indiana and other states.[13] A survey of cases found that the Oregon Supreme Court referred in its opinions more often to Indiana's constitution than to any other state's, with neighboring California as a close second.[14]

B. Interpreting Other Constitutional Provisions and Amendments

The Oregon Supreme Court uses a different methodology for interpreting provisions and amendments of the constitution that were adopted after 1859. The Oregon Constitution can be amended in two ways. In the traditional method, the legislature passes an amendment that is voted on by the voters of the state.[15] The second method is the initiative process,[16] which may be unfamiliar to some readers.

The initiative process was adopted in 1902 in response to legislative corruption.[17] The initiative process allows voters to propose amendments to the state constitution by placing measures on the election ballot. Voters begin the process by submitting a petition with at least a certain number of signatures of qualified voters; this number is equal to eight percent of the votes cast for governor in the preceding election. The number of signatures required in 2002 to place a constitutional amendment on the ballot was 89,048. The initiative

---

13. 5 Or. L. Rev. 200 (1925–1926).

14. Patrick Baude, *Interstate Dialogue in State Constitutional Law*, 28 Rutgers L.J. 835, 838, 859 (1997).

15. Or. Const., Art. XVII.

16. Or. Const., Art. IV, § 1; *see also State Initiative and Referendum Manual*, Or. Sec. of St. (available at www.sos.state.or.us/elections/Publications/pub.htm).

17. *See* David Schuman, *The Origin of State Constitutional Direct Democracy: William Simon U'Ren and "The Oregon System,"* 67 Temple L. Rev. 947, 948–49 (1994).

petition must clear other procedural hurdles before being presented to the voters in the next election.

In interpreting amendments to the Oregon Constitution, the Court's goal is to determine the intent of the voters.

The best evidence of the voters' intent is the text of the provision itself. The context of the language of the ballot measure may also be considered; however, if the intent is clear based on the text and context of the constitutional provision, the court does not look further.[18]

If the voters' intent is not clear from the text and context of the provision, the court examines the history of the provision.[19] This history includes "the ballot title and arguments for and against the measure included in the voters' pamphlet, and contemporaneous news reports and editorial comment on the measure."[20] This historical material is available from the Elections Division for about six years after a provision is adopted; voters' pamphlets from 1995 forward are available online at www.sos.state.or.us/elections/Publications/onlinevp.htm. After about six years, the information is available from the State Archives. Some of this material is also available on the microfiche set *State Constitutional Conventions*.

Although the initiative process remains an integral part of Oregon law, criticism of problems inherent with this system exists. One criticism is that voters vote to decrease taxes and increase spending at the same time.[21] Additionally, the ease by which the state constitution may be amended raises concerns that the Oregon Constitution will become a "museum of unrelated laws enshrining the temporary po-

---

18. *Roseburg Sch. Dist. v. City of Roseburg*, 316 Or. 374, 378 (1993); *see also Stranahan v. Fred Meyer, Inc.*, 331 Or. 38, 58 n. 13 (2000) (stating the Supreme Court's intention to apply this methodology to "constitutional provisions and amendments adopted by legislative referral").

19. *Ecumenical Ministries of Oregon v. Oregon St. Lottery*, 318 Or. 551, 559 (1994).

20. *Id.* at 559 n. 8.

21. Hans A. Linde, *On Reconstituting "Republican Government,"* 19 Okla. City U. L. Rev. 193, 204 (1994).

litical preoccupations of... [the] times."[22] However, the initiative system also enables Oregon voters themselves to improve the process, as happened when they voted to prohibit payment based on the number of signatures obtained on initiative petitions.[23]

A useful resource in understanding these processes is entitled *State Initiative, Referendum, and Recall Manual,* which is provided by the Oregon Secretary of State. It is available in hard copy and also may be downloaded from www.sos.state.or.us/elections/Publications/pub.htm.[24] The manual provides descriptions of the overall process as well as step-by-step instructions and examples of required forms.

Additionally, the *Oregon Blue Book,* the official state directory which is compiled and published in odd-numbered years by the Secretary of State, contains a comprehensive listing of initiatives and referenda organized by election dates, measure numbers, ballot titles, and the resulting tally of "Yes" and "No" votes. An electronic version of the *Oregon Blue Book* is available online at www.bluebook.state.or.us, as well as through www.sos.state.or.us.

III. United States Constitution

The federal constitution is published along with the Oregon Constitution in *Oregon Revised Statutes.* There is an index immediately following the federal constitution. It is also available in print in the first few volumes of *United States Code Annotated* and *United States*

---

22. David B. Frohnmayer & Hans A. Linde, *Appendix: Initiating "Laws" in the Form of "Constitutional Amendments": An Amicus Curiae Brief,* 34 Willamette L. Rev. 749, 773 (1998). As Justice Gillette stated, "Constitutional amendments should be made of sterner stuff." Michael Gillette, *The Legislative Function: Initiative and Referendum,* 67 Or. L. Rev. 55, 62 (1988).

23. *See* November 5, 2002 Election Date, Measure 26: Amends Constitution: Prohibits Payment, Receipt of Payment Based on the Number of Initiative, Referendum Petition Signatures Obtained (available at www.bluebook. state.or.us/state/elections/elections22a.htm).

24. Unlike the hard copy version, the current electronic version is divided into the *State Initiative and Referendum Manual* and the *Recall Manual.*

Code Service. Although these series are primarily used to research federal statutes, the publishers include the United States Constitution as a convenience for readers. These series are explained in Chapter 5. Additionally, publications of other states' codes may include the United States Constitution, just as ORS does.

The United States Constitution is also available online at both state and federal websites. Some addresses of relevant sites include:

- www.leg.state.or.us/billsset.htm, which includes an index;
- www.house.gov/Constitution/Constitution.html, which is linked to the U.S. House of Representatives site but does not provide an index;
- www.law.emory.edu/FEDERAL/usconst.html, a university site that provides a search engine.

Chapter 3

Judicial Opinions and Reporters

A judicial opinion, also called a case, is written by a court to explain its decision in a particular dispute. Cases are published in rough chronological order in books called *reporters*.[1] Some reporters include only cases decided by a certain court, for example, the Oregon Supreme Court. Other reporters include cases from courts within a specific geographic region, for example, the western United States. Still other reporters publish only those cases that deal with a certain topic, such as bankruptcy, media law, or rules of civil and criminal procedure.[2] Reporters that publish cases from a particular court or geographic area are the most commonly used by general practitioners and are the focus of this chapter.

I. Reporters for Oregon Cases

All cases decided by the Oregon Supreme Court are published in *Oregon Reports*. The abbreviation for this reporter is "Or." The case *State v. Warner*, 298 Or. 640 (1985),[3] can be found in volume 298 of

---

1. Digests, tools that index cases by topic, are covered in Chapter 4.

2. Some of these topical reporters are discussed in Part III of this chapter.

3. Under Oregon courts' rules for citation, no periods are used in reporter abbreviations. This rule differs from other states' citation rules and from the national citation systems, as explained in Appendix A. For courts in Oregon, the cite for the *Warner* case would be 298 Or 640 (1985).

the series *Oregon Reports*, starting on page 640. The case was decided in 1985.

Oregon's intermediate appellate court opinions are published in a separate reporter called *Oregon Reports, Court of Appeals*. "Or. App." is the abbreviation for this reporter. The case *State v. Reid*, 36 Or. App. 417 (1978), was published in volume 36 of the reporter series *Oregon Reports, Court of Appeals*, beginning on page 417. It was decided in 1978. Almost all opinions of the Court of Appeals are published.[4]

Oregon has a separate court that addresses matters of taxation. The decisions of the Oregon Tax Court are reported in *Oregon Tax Reports*, abbreviated "OTR."

Cases from state trial courts in Oregon are not published; in fact, few states publish opinions at the trial court level. Unpublished opinions may be obtained directly from the court that decided the case.

Oregon Reports and *Oregon Reports, Court of Appeals* are the official reporters for Oregon appellate cases. Cases from these courts are also reported in a commercially produced regional reporter called *Pacific Reporter*. While the text of the court's opinion is the same in the official and unofficial reporters, the appearance, pagination, and editorial additions may be different.

Commercial reporters often combine several courts' opinions under a single title. *Pacific Reporter* publishes cases from the courts of the following fifteen states: Alaska, Arizona, California, Colorado, Hawaii, Idaho, Kansas, Montana, Nevada, New Mexico, Oklahoma, Oregon, Utah, Washington, and Wyoming.[5] *Pacific Reporter* includes cases from the intermediate and highest appellate courts of most of

---

4. Sometimes the Court of Appeals affirms a case without writing an opinion; these cases are "affirmed without opinion" and are referred to as "AWOPs." They are listed in a table in *Oregon Reports, Court of Appeals* but should not be cited.

5. If a state does not publish its own reporter, the regional reporter may be the official reporter. For example, the official reporter of Alaska cases is *Pacific Reporter*. The publisher, West, also publishes an offprint of *Pacific Reporter* that contains only Alaska cases. It is called *Alaska Reporter*. The appearance, pagination, and editorial aids are exactly like those in *Pacific Reporter*, but the volumes contain only those pages that report cases from Alaska courts.

these states.[6] Other regional reporters are *North Eastern Reporter, Atlantic Reporter, South Eastern Reporter, Southern Reporter, South Western Reporter*, and *North Western Reporter*. All of these regional reporters are published by West. Because publishers decide which states to group together in regional reporters, these groupings have no legal impact.

The coverage of each regional reporter is not the same as the composition of the federal circuits explained in Chapter 1. The Ninth Circuit includes Alaska, Arizona, California, Hawaii, Idaho, Montana, Nevada, Oregon, and Washington, as well as Guam and the Northern Mariana Islands. It does not include Colorado, Kansas, New Mexico, Oklahoma, Utah, or Wyoming, yet those states' cases are reported in *Pacific Reporter*.

Sometimes when a reporter reaches a certain volume number, the publisher begins another *series*. In 1931, after volume 300 of *Pacific Reporter* was published, the publisher decided to begin again with volume one of *Pacific Reporter, Second Series*. In 2000, following publication of volume 999 in the second series, a third series was started, *Pacific Reporter, Third Series*. To find a case in a reporter with multiple series, you must know which series the case was reported in.

While attorneys practicing strictly in Oregon would be likely to subscribe to *Oregon Reports* and *Oregon Reports, Court of Appeals*, attorneys working frequently with the laws of multiple states would be more likely to subscribe to *Pacific Reporter* or another regional reporter. When writing a memo or brief, if no rule or custom dictates that you must cite to a specific reporter, cite to the reporter that others reading your document are most likely to have. Often that will be the West regional reporter listed above. If you were writing a memo for a firm in Seattle, for example, you would cite the Oregon cases mentioned above in *Pacific Reporter, Second Series*. To indicate which state's courts decided the cases, include an abbreviation at the beginning of the date parenthetical.

---

6. Since 1960, opinions of California's intermediate appellate courts have been published in *California Reporter*, not in *Pacific Reporter*.

EXAMPLE: *State v. Warner*, 696 P.2d 1052 (Or. 1985).

State v. Reid, 585 P.2d 411 (Or. App. 1978).

If you are not sure which reporter your reader may have access to, you may want to include citations to both reporters. Two citations that refer to the same case in different reporters are called *parallel citations*.

EXAMPLE: *State v. Warner*, 298 Or. 640, 696 P.2d 1052 (1985).

State v. Reid, 36 Or. App. 417, 585 P.2d 411 (1978).

A. The Anatomy of a Reported Case

A case printed in a reporter contains the exact language of the court's opinion. Additionally, the publisher adds supplemental information intended to aid researchers in learning about the case, locating the relevant parts of the case, and finding similar cases. Some of these research aids are gleaned from the court record of the case while others are written by the publisher's editorial staff. The following discussion explains the information and enhancements included in *Oregon Reports*. Most reporters will include most of these items, though perhaps in a different order. To best understand the following discussion, select from the library shelves a volume of *Oregon Reports*, preferably a volume containing a case you are familiar with. Alternatively, refer to the case excerpt in Table 3-1 for examples of the concepts explained below. Note that this excerpt is from a case published by the state, not by West, so editorial enhancements are slightly different from those in *Pacific Reporter*.

Dates. Each case begins with the date the case was argued and submitted to the court, and the date of the court's decision. For citation purposes, only the year the case was decided is important.

Parties and procedural designations. All of the parties are listed with their procedural designations. In general, if a losing party has a right to appeal, she will be called the *appellant* and the opposing party will be called the *respondent.*[7] If the losing party must ask the

---

7. In other jurisdictions, the term appellee is used for respondent in this situation.

Table 3-1. Case Excerpt
State v. Warner, 298 Or. 640 (1985)

Argued and submitted July 10, 1984, reversed and remanded
February 20, reconsideration denied March 26, 1985 ◄——— Dates

STATE OF OREGON,
Respondent on Review, ◄——————— Parties and
v. procedural
FOREST DWAINE WARNER, designations
Petitioner on Review. Docket
(10-28-02595; CA A25336; SC S30596) ◄——— numbers

696 P2d 1052 ◄——————— Parallel cite

Defendant was convicted in Circuit Court, Lane
County, Maurice K. Merten, J., of burglary in the first
degree. The Court of Appeals affirmed, 67 Or App 251,
677 P2d 733. On review from the Court of Appeals, the
Supreme Court, Roberts, J., held that a metal signpost was ◄ Synopsis
not a burglar's tool so as to render defendant vulnerable to
the charge of burglary in the first degree.

Reversed and remanded for entry of judgment of
conviction of burglary in the second degree, and for
resentencing for that crime.

**1. Burglary — Offenses and responsibility therefor —
Possession of burglars' tools**

In view of fact that first degree burglary statute containing
cross-reference to definition in possession statute was
approved by both houses after it left senate committee,
burglar's tools were to be defined consistently in first degree ◄ Headnote
burglary statute and in possession statute, regardless of any
narrower intent by senate committee which drafted language
in burglary statute. ORS 164.215, 164.235.

**2. Burglary — Offenses and responsibility therefor —
Possession of burglars' tools**

Alternative legitimate use does not eliminate object
from category of potential burglar's tools. ORS 164.235.

Source: *Oregon Reports.* Reprinted with permission of West, a Thomson
business.

court to review the case, he is the *petitioner* and the opposing party will be the *respondent*.

Docket numbers. The number assigned to the case by a court is called a docket number. Each court will assign a different docket number to the case. Docket numbers are helpful in locating the parties' briefs, a court's orders, or other documents related to that case. Because some of these documents are not published, they can be obtained only from the court that decided the case. To request these documents, you must have the appropriate docket number or, in some instances, the parties' names.

Parallel cites. Often publishers will provide citations to other reporters that have published the same case. The text of an opinion reported at parallel cites is identical, although some of the editorial enhancements may be different.

Synopsis. One of the most helpful research aids included by the publishers is a synopsis. This is a short summary of the key facts, procedure, legal points, and disposition of the case. Reading a synopsis can quickly tell you whether a case is on point. You cannot rely exclusively on a synopsis; at least skim each case to determine whether it is important for your research. Moreover, you must never cite the synopsis, even when it gives an excellent summary of the case, since it is not authoritative.

Headnotes. A headnote is a sentence or short paragraph that sets out a single point of law in a case. Most cases will have several headnotes. The text of each headnote often comes directly from the text of the opinion. But because only the opinion itself is authoritative, do not rely on headnotes in doing research and do not cite them in legal documents. At the beginning of each headnote is a number identifying it in sequence with other headnotes. Within the text of the opinion, the same sequence number will appear in bold print[8] at the point in the text supporting the headnote. You should read and cite that text, not the headnote.

---

8. In some reporters, including *Pacific Reporter*, these numbers are not bold but are enclosed in brackets.

Just after the sequence number, each headnote begins with a word or phrase, or several words and phrases, in bold print. These words and phrases are used in subject indexes to locate other cases that discuss similar points of law.

Headnotes are generally the product of a given reporter's editorial staff, even when the text of the headnote is identical to language used in the opinion. Thus, the number of headnotes — and the text of the headnotes — may differ depending on which publisher's reporter is being used. Fortunately in Oregon, the headnotes of the official reporters and the headnotes of West's *Pacific Reporter* are essentially the same.

Library references. Some reporters, including *Oregon Reports*, give cross references to the relevant sections of a legal encyclopedia like *Corpus Juris Secundum* (C.J.S.). A summary of the law in a legal encyclopedia could provide valuable background information and refer to additional cases or statutes that are on point.

Procedural information. *Oregon Reports* volumes contain a variety of procedural information. For example, those volumes indicate when a case was decided *per curiam*, meaning that no judge is given credit as author of the court's opinion. Other procedural information includes the court from which the case was appealed, the judges who heard the case, and the judge who wrote the decision. Note that following a judge's name will be "C.J." for the chief judge (or "P.J." for the presiding judge in the Court of Appeals) or "J." for another judge. If a case includes concurring or dissenting opinions, they will be noted in the procedural listings. Also in this section will be the attorneys who argued for each party.

Disposition. The disposition of the case is the court's decision to affirm, reverse, remand, or vacate the decision below. If the appellate court agrees with only part of the lower court's decision, the appellate court may affirm in part and reverse in part.

Opinion. In *Oregon Reports*, the actual opinion of the court begins on a new page, with the name of the judge who wrote the opinion given in bold.

If the judges who heard the case do not agree on the outcome or the reasons for the outcome, there may be several opinions. The opinion supported by a majority of the judges is called the *majority opinion*. An opinion written to agree with the outcome but not the reasoning of the majority is called a *concurring opinion*. Opinions written by judges who disagree with the outcome supported by the majority of the judges are called *dissenting opinions*. While only the majority opinion is binding precedent, the other opinions provide valuable insights and may be cited as persuasive authority. If there is no majority on both the outcome and the reasoning, the case will be decided by whichever opinion garners the most support, and is called a *plurality decision*.

Cases decided by intermediate courts of appeals are heard by three judges sitting as a *panel* of the full court. If a party does not agree with the decision of the panel, it may ask for a rehearing *en banc*, meaning that all of the judges on that court would rehear the case.

B. Tables in Reporters

Each volume of *Oregon Reports* contains several helpful tables. Judges serving on the Supreme Court or circuit courts during the time of the cases reported in each volume are listed in tables at the front of the volume. *Oregon Reports, Court of Appeals* provides the names of the judges on the Court of Appeals and circuit courts.

There is also an alphabetical listing of all the cases reported in each volume. In *Oregon Reports*, it is followed by an alphabetical list of petitions for review that were decided. The court rarely issues opinions when it grants, denies, or dismisses these petitions. Each case is simply listed in a table within the reporter. While most petitions for review by the Oregon Supreme Court are denied, denying a petition does not mean that the court agrees with the outcome or analysis in the lower court's opinion.

At the back of each reporter is a subject index. The words or phrases given in bold at the beginning of each headnote are included in the index. Searching the index for these words and phrases and for other relevant terms can point you to additional cases that are on point. Chapter 4 explains how to use *digests* to find cases in other reporters on the same topic.

C. Advance Sheets

The bound volumes of reporters can take months to be published. To make cases available sooner, publishers supply subscribers with *advance sheets*. These are softbound booklets, which can be published much more quickly than hardbound books. Advance sheets for *Oregon Reports* and *Oregon Reports, Court of Appeals* are published every two weeks.

The advance sheets for Oregon include cases from the Supreme Court and the Court of Appeals in one booklet.[9] The spine of each booklet is numbered, beginning with the first issue in January. Note that the January issue will report cases decided during December of the previous year.

The pagination used in the advance sheets is the same as will be used in the hardbound volumes; thus, a cite to a case in the advance sheets will still be accurate after the case is published in hardbound volumes. This is possible because the title of the case appears on the first page of the case's cite, an extra page is left open for the synopsis, headnotes, and other enhancements, and the text of the case begins on a new page. When a case has more headnotes than will fit in the allotted space, the hardbound volumes include extra pages with letter suffixes. Inserting these extra page numbers allows the same pagination in the text of the case and in subsequent cases.

> EXAMPLE: The case *State v. Lyons*, 161 Or. App. 355 (1999), begins on page 355. The headnotes and other editorial information appear on pages 356, 356-a, and 356-b. The court's opinion begins on page 357, just as it did in the advance sheets.

To allow this uniform pagination between advance sheets and bound reporters, the sections of the Oregon advance sheets are paginated independently. The section containing Oregon Supreme Court cases continues the pagination from the previous advance sheet for Supreme Court cases. Similarly, the section containing Court of Ap-

---

9. Decisions of the Oregon Tax Court are also included.

peals cases continues the pagination from the previous advance sheet for Court of Appeals cases. An advance sheet section begins numbering with page one when a new hardbound volume is anticipated.

Advance sheets contain more than just cases. Each advance sheet contains a table of cases and a list of petitions for review. Advance sheets also contain the same type of subject index as the bound reporters, though in the advance sheet the index will appear before the cases, rather than at the back of the book. Additionally, advance sheets report court orders relating to such things as the Code of Judicial Conduct, Rules of Procedure, and Rules for Admission of Attorneys. Advance sheet pages containing these types of materials are enclosed in brackets to distinguish them from the pages that will be included in the bound reporter volumes.

D. Other Sources for Finding Oregon Cases

To provide access to cases even faster than advance sheets can be published, *slip opinions* are available either from the court that decided the case or online at www.publications.ojd.state.or.us. A slip opinion is the actual document produced by the court, without the editorial enhancements normally added by the publisher. This means that it will appear different from the printed versions in both *Oregon Reports* and *Pacific Reporter*. The state website is updated weekly.

Additionally, Willamette University College of Law provides an online service called Willamette Law Online at www.willamette.edu/wucl/wlo/. This service provides summaries of Oregon Supreme Court and Court of Appeals decisions as well as summaries of cases from the United States Supreme Court, the Ninth Circuit Court of Appeals, and the highest courts of Washington, California, and Alaska. While informative, these summaries should not be cited as legal authority.

II. Reporters for Federal Cases

So far this chapter has dealt with reporters for Oregon and other states. This part explains the reporters for cases decided by our fed-

Table 3-2. Reporters for Federal Court Cases

Court	Reporter Name	Abbreviation
U.S. Supreme Court	*United States Reports* (official)	U.S.
	Supreme Court Reporter	S. Ct.
	United States Supreme Court Reports, Lawyers' Edition	L. Ed. or L. Ed. 2d
U.S. Courts of Appeals	*Federal Reporter*	F. or F.2d or F.3d
U.S. District Courts	*Federal Supplement*	F. Supp. or F. Supp. 2d

eral courts. Table 3-2 lists the federal court reporters, along with their citation abbreviations.

A. United States Supreme Court

Decisions of the United States Supreme Court are reported in *United States Reports*, which is the official reporter; *Supreme Court Reporter*, which is a West publication; and *United States Supreme Court Reports, Lawyers' Edition*, another unofficial reporter now in its second series. Although *United States Reports* is the official reporter, meaning that you should cite it if possible, that series frequently publishes cases several years after they are decided. Even the advance sheets can run several years late. Thus, for recent cases, you will often cite the *Supreme Court Reporter*. Another source for finding recent cases from the Supreme Court is *United States Law Week*. This service publishes the full text of cases from the Supreme Court and provides summaries of important decisions of state and federal courts.

There are a number of online sources for Supreme Court opinions. The Court's website at www.supremecourtus.gov/opinions/opinions. html includes slip opinions soon after the decisions are rendered. An educational site supported by Cornell University also provides decisions quickly. The address is http://supct.law.cornell.edu/supct/.

B. United States Courts of Appeals

Cases decided by the federal intermediate appellate courts are published in *Federal Reporter*, now in its third series. The abbreviations for these reporters are F., F.2d, and F.3d. Some Court of Appeals cases that were not selected for publication in *Federal Reporter*, and are not precedential, may be published in a relatively new reporter series, *Federal Appendix*. Limited access to recent opinions is available on the U.S. Courts website at www.uscourts.gov and the Cornell website at www.law.cornell.edu/federal/opinions.html.

C. United States District Courts

Selected cases from the United States District Courts, the federal trial courts, are reported in *Federal Supplement* and *Federal Supplement, Second Series*. The citation abbreviations for these reporters are F. Supp. and F. Supp. 2d. Some opinions are available on the U.S. Courts and Cornell websites as well.

III. Topical Reporters

Some reporters publish cases on a particular topic, rather than cases from a specific court or region. For example, *Federal Rules Decisions* includes federal trial court cases that analyze federal rules of civil and criminal procedure. Similarly, *Bankruptcy Reporter* includes cases from federal courts on that topic. Both of these reporters are published by West, so they will contain West's editorial enhancements. Other publishers also provide reporters in topical areas. An example is *Media Law Reporter*, which publishes all relevant opinions of the United States Supreme Court as well as significant opinions of federal and state courts on the topic of media law.

IV. Reading and Analyzing Cases

Once you locate a case, you must read it, understand it, and analyze its potential relevance to the problem you are researching. An attorney, judge, or client who has asked you to do the research will not be satisfied if you return from the library with a stack of photocopied cases you have not yet analyzed.

Do not expect reading a case to be easy. Understanding a case may take more mental work than you have ever dedicated to a few pages. It is not unusual for beginning lawyers to read complex cases at around fifteen pages per hour. Often this reading is interrupted by referring to a law dictionary to try to understand the terms used. Early efforts will be more productive if you have a basic understanding of civil procedure terms and the fundamental aspects of case analysis, then follow the strategies outlined at the end of this chapter.

A. A Thimbleful of Civil Procedure

The person who believes he was harmed begins civil litigation by filing a *complaint* in the court he selects. The *plaintiff* is the person who files the complaint; the person against whom the complaint is filed is the *defendant*. The complaint names the parties, states the facts, notes the relevant laws, and asks for relief. Courts vary considerably in how much information is required at this stage of the litigation. In general, the complaint must be specific enough to put the defendant on notice of the legal concerns at issue and to allow her to prepare a defense. In Oregon, more specific pleading is required.

The defendant has a limited amount of time in which to file a response to this complaint. (If the defendant does nothing within the prescribed time, the plaintiff can ask the court for a *default judgment*, which would grant the plaintiff the relief sought in the complaint.) One form of response to the complaint is an *answer*. In the answer, the defendant admits to the parts of the complaint that she knows are true, denies those things that she disputes, and asserts no knowledge of other allegations. The defendant also may raise affirmative defenses.

Throughout the litigation, parties submit a variety of papers to the court for its consideration. Some require no action or response from the court, for example, the filing of the complaint. In other instances, a party asks the court to make a decision or take action. An example is a motion for summary judgment, where a party asks the court to decide in that party's favor without the need for a trial.

When the trial judge grants a motion that ends a case, the losing party can appeal. The appealing party is called the *appellant*; the other party is the *respondent*.[10] In deciding an appeal from an order granting a motion, the appellate court is deciding whether the trial judge was correct in issuing the order at that stage of the litigation. If the appellate court agrees with the decision of the trial judge, it will *affirm*. If not, the court will *reverse* the order granting the motion and in some instances *remand* the case back to the trial court.

Even at trial, the parties might make motions that can be appealed. For example, during the trial, the plaintiff presents his evidence first. After all of the plaintiff's witnesses have testified, the defendant may move for a *judgment as a matter of law*, arguing that the plaintiff cannot win based on the evidence presented and asking for an immediate decision. An order granting that motion could be appealed. Double jeopardy?

Most of the reported cases are appeals of orders granting motions. These cases apply different standards of review, depending on the motion that is the object of the appeal. While standards of review are beyond the scope of this book, understanding the procedural posture of the case is crucial to understanding the court's holding. The relevant rules of civil procedure will guide your analysis. Texts listed in Appendix B of this book contain helpful explanations as well.

---

10. In most jurisdictions, the terms appellant-appellee are used when a party has a right to appeal, while the terms petitioner-respondent apply to parties when the court has discretion to hear the appeal. Oregon uses the term respondent for the non-moving party in both instances.

B. Analyzing the Substance of Cases

Early in your career it may be difficult to determine whether a case is relevant to your research problem. If the case concerns the same legally significant facts as your client's situation and the court applies law on point for your problem, then the case is relevant. Legally significant facts are those that affect the court's decision. Some attorneys call these outcome-determinative facts or key facts. Which facts are legally significant depends on the case. The height of the defendant in a contract dispute is unlikely to be legally significant, but that fact may be critical in a criminal case where the only eye witness testified that the thief was about five feet tall.

Rarely will your research reveal a case with facts that are exactly the same as your client's situation. Rather, several cases may involve facts that are similar to your client's situation but not exactly the same. Your job is to determine whether the facts are similar enough for a court to apply the law in the same way and reach the same outcome. If the court reached a decision favorable to your client, you will highlight the similarities. If, on the other hand, the court reached an unfavorable decision from your client's perspective, you may argue that the case is distinguishable from yours based on its facts or that its reasoning is faulty. You have an ethical duty to ensure that the court knows about a case directly on point, even if the outcome of that case is adverse to your client.

Table 3-3. Analyzing Cases

	Favorable Case	Unfavorable Case
Facts	Highlight similarities	Stress differences
Law	Apply reasoning	Distinguish reasoning

You are also unlikely to find one case that addresses all aspects of your client's situation. Most legal claims have several elements or factors. *Elements* are required subparts of a claim, while *factors* are important aspects but not required. If a court decides that one element is not met, it may not discuss others. In a different case, the court may decide that two factors are so overwhelming that others have no impact on the outcome. In these circumstances, you would have to find other cases that analyze the other elements or factors.

Once you determine that a case is relevant to some portion of your analysis, you must decide how heavily it will weigh in your analysis. Two important points need to be considered here. One is the concept of *stare decisis;* the other is the difference between the holding of the case and dicta within that case.

Stare decisis means "to stand by things decided."[11] This means that courts must follow prior opinions, ensuring consistency in the application of the law. This requirement, however, is limited to the courts within one jurisdiction. The Court of Appeals of Oregon must follow the decisions of the Oregon Supreme Court, but not those of the courts of any other state. The concept of *stare decisis* also refers to a court with respect to its own opinions. The Court of Appeals, thus, should follow its own earlier cases in deciding new matters. If a court decides not to continue following its earlier cases, it is usually because of changes in society that have outdated the law of the earlier case, or because a new statute has been enacted that changes the legal landscape.

Under *stare decisis*, courts are required to follow the holding of prior cases. The holding is the court's ultimate decision on the matter of law at issue in the case. Other statements or observations included in the opinion are not binding; they are referred to as *dicta.* For example, a court in a property dispute may hold that the land belongs to X. In reaching that decision, the court may note that had the facts been slightly different, it would have decided the land belonged to Y. That observation is not binding on future courts, though it may be cited as persuasive authority.

After finding a number of cases that have similar facts, that discuss the same legal issue, and that are binding on your client, the next step is to synthesize the cases to state and explain the legal rule. Sometimes a court states the rule fully; if not, piece together the information

11. *Black's Law Dictionary* 1414 (Bryan A. Garner ed., 7th ed., West 1999).

from the relevant cases to state the rule completely but concisely. Then use the analysis and facts of various cases to explain the law. Decide how the rule applies to the client's facts, and determine your conclusion. Note that this method of synthesis is much more than mere summaries of all the various cases. Legal analysis texts in Appendix B of this book explain synthesis in detail.

C. Strategies for Reading Cases

As you begin reading cases, the following strategies may help you understand them more quickly and more thoroughly.

- Review the synopsis quickly to determine whether the case seems to be on point. If so, skim the headnotes to find the particular portion of the case that is relevant. Remember that one case may discuss several issues of law, only one or two of which may interest you. Go to the portion of the case identified by the relevant headnote and decide whether it is important for your project.
- If so, skim the entire case to get a feeling for what happened and why, focusing on the portion of the case identified by the relevant headnote.
- Read the case slowly and carefully. Skip the parts that are obviously not pertinent to your problem. For example, if you are researching a property question, there is no need to scrutinize the tort issue that is not pertinent to your property question.
- At the end of each paragraph or page, consider what you have read. If you cannot summarize it, try reading the material again.
- The next time you read the case, take notes. The notes may be in the form of a formal "case brief" or they may be scribbles that only you can understand. Regardless of the form, the process of taking notes will help you parse through, identify, and comprehend the essential concepts of the case. In law school, the notes will record your understanding of the case both for class discussion and for the end of the semester when you begin to review for exams. When preparing to write a legal document, the notes will assist you in organizing your analysis into an outline.

- Note that skimming text online or highlighting a printed page is often not sufficient to achieve thorough comprehension of judicial opinions.

Chapter 4

Digests

A digest is a multi-volume index in which cases are organized by subject. Under each subject, the digest provides a headnote from each case that addresses that particular subject and a citation to the case. The digest does not reprint the entire case. Digests are important research tools because reporters organize cases chronologically, rather than by subject. Although most research texts explain digests after reporters, you will turn to digests first in your research process.

I. West Digests

This chapter concentrates on digests published by West because they are the most widely used. Much of the information provided here would apply to any other case digest as well.

The scope of most West digests is based on jurisdiction.[1] The current digest used for researching Oregon law is *Oregon Digest 2d*. It includes headnotes of cases from state and federal courts in Oregon. Headnotes from cases that originated in Oregon and were later decided by the Ninth Circuit and the United States Supreme Court are indexed here, too. This digest also includes references to Oregon Tax Court cases, opinions of the Oregon Attorney General, and articles published by Oregon law reviews. An example of entries in *Oregon Digest 2d* is given in Table 4-1.

---

1. Some digests are limited by topic, such as *Bankruptcy Digest* and *Military Justice Digest*.

Table 4-1. Excerpts from *Oregon Digest 2d* "Adverse Possession"

Or. 1999. To succeed on adverse possession claims, claimants must establish, by clear and convincing evidence, that the use of the property was actual, open, notorious, exclusive, continuous, and hostile for a 10-year period.

Hoffman v. Freeman Land and Timber, LLC., 994 P.2d 106, 329 Or. 554.

Or. App. 1993. "Hostile" for adverse possession purposes means that claimant possessed property intending to be its owner and not in subordination to true owner. ORS 12.050.

Schoeller v. Kulawiak, 848 P.2d 619, 118 Or.App. 524, review denied 858 P.2d 1314, 317 Or. 272.

Or. App. 1989. Term "hostile," as term is used in context of adverse possession, means that claimant possesses property intending to be its owner and not in subordination to true owner; possession of realty under mistaken belief of ownership normally satisfies element of hostility without need for inquiry into claimant's subjective intent, but belief must result from pure mistake, rather than mistake based upon conscious doubt.

Knapp v. Daily, 772 P.2d 1363, 96 Or.App. 327.

Source: *Oregon Digest 2d.* Reprinted with permission of West, a Thomson business.

Some digests index cases from a number of different jurisdictions. For instance, *Pacific Digest* contains headnotes of cases that are reported in *Pacific Reporter*, which were decided by many different state courts. Note that a regional digest like *Pacific Digest* will not index federal cases. Another digest, *Federal Practice Digest*, provides an index to cases decided by federal trial and appellate courts. The full text of those cases is published in *Federal Supplement*, *Federal Reporter*, and the various reporters for United States Supreme Court cases.[2]

---

2. West publishes a digest for United States Supreme Court cases called *United States Supreme Court Digest*. Another digest for those cases is *United States Supreme Court Digest, Lawyers' Edition*. Note that the *Lawyers' Edition* classification scheme is not identical to the West system. Be careful not to confuse the headnotes of one publisher with those of another publisher.

Oregon Digest 2d is cumulative, including cases from 1843 to the present; it replaced the first edition. Many other digests are not cumulative. For example, *Federal Practice Digest 4th* includes headnotes of cases published from the mid-1980s through the present. The previous series, *Federal Practice Digest 3d*, included cases from 1975 through the mid-1980s. Similarly, *Pacific Digest* publishes bound sets periodically; the most recent includes cases reported in volume 585 of *Pacific Reporter, Second Series* and subsequent volumes. To do thorough research in *Federal Practice Digest* and in *Pacific Digest*, you may need to consult more than one series. Consider the period of time that is pertinent for your research, and then check the introductory information at the front of each digest to determine whether the digest covers that period.

A. Topics and Key Numbers

Oregon Digest 2d, *Pacific Digest*, *Federal Practice Digest*, and other West digests index cases according to the West system of *topics* and *key numbers*. West assigns a topic and key number to each headnote in a case, based on the legal point that is the focus of the headnote. The West *topic* places the headnote within a broad subject area of the law. Examples of West topics include "Criminal Law," "Health and Environment," and "Zoning and Planning." The *key number* relates to a subtopic within that area of law.[3] An example of a topic-key number for cases dealing with criminal evidence is "Criminal Law 338(1)."[4] The key number 338(1) refers to the subtopic "Evidence—Facts in Issue and Relevance."

"Criminal Law" is a vast topic, containing over 1,000 key numbers on subtopics covering criminal intent, defenses, pleas, trials, and sen-

---

3. The topics and key numbers are synonymous with the subject index entries in *Oregon Reports*, discussed in Chapter 3, Part IB.
4. Some headnotes have parentheses and some have decimal points. In general, the parentheses are used for subheadings while decimals are used to insert new key numbers. Moreover, a topic outline may omit a key number that is no longer used.

tencing guidelines. As an example of a much shorter topic, "Theatres and Shows" includes just a few key numbers on subtopics addressing licenses, admission, and liability for injuries to those attending.

B. Headnotes

The digest entries under each topic-key number are the actual headnotes found in cases. West has assigned each headnote a topic-key number. Each case is indexed in the digest under as many topics and key numbers as it had headnotes in the reporter.[5]

The bulk of each headnote entry is a sentence that summarizes the point of law that is the specific subject of the topic-key number assigned to that headnote. Although the language is usually copied directly from the text of the case, headnotes are not authoritative and should never be cited.

In a digest, headnotes are arranged under each topic-key number according to the court that decided the case. Federal cases are listed first, followed by state court cases. Within the federal and state systems, cases are listed according to judicial hierarchy: cases from the highest appellate court are listed first, followed by decisions of intermediate appellate courts, then trial court cases. Cases from each court are given in reverse chronological order. This order is helpful because recent cases, which are listed first, are more likely to be pertinent to your research.

At the beginning of each headnote is a court abbreviation and date. The abbreviations are explained in tables at the beginning of each digest volume. Some of the court abbreviations used in *Oregon Digest 2d* headnotes are noted in Table 4-2, in the order in which they would have appeared under one topic-key number.

At the end of the digest headnote are citations to any statutes that are cited in the case. This information is followed by the case citation and any parallel citations.

---

5. Although cases published in *Oregon Tax Reports* do not receive topic-key numbers, some are included in *Oregon Digest 2d* as "Library References" under topic-key numbers that are relevant to the subject matter of the case.

Table 4-2. Court Abbreviations in *Oregon Digest 2d*

C.A.9 (Or.) 1980.	A 1980 case that originated in the federal district court in Oregon and was decided by the Ninth Circuit Court of Appeals.*
D.Or. 1982.	A 1982 case decided by the federal district court in Oregon.
Or. 2001.	A 2001 case decided by the Supreme Court of Oregon.
Or.App. 1989.	A 1989 case decided by the Oregon Court of Appeals.
Law Rev. 1988.	A 1988 article from an Oregon law review.
Atty.Gen. 1975	A 1975 opinion from the Oregon Attorney General.

* The abbreviations in these tables at the front of each volume are not always identical to those used in the digest headnotes. For example, the digest table includes "C.A.Or." for the United States Court of Appeals. The digest headnotes actually use the abbreviation "C.A.9 (Or.)" for that court.

Although West may have assigned a topic-key number to a particular point of law, a given jurisdiction may not have decided a case on that point. In that instance, no entries will appear under the topic-key number of that jurisdiction's digest. However, the topic-key number system makes it easy to research cases in other jurisdictions using West digests, which may lead to persuasive authorities.

II. Digest Research

There are several approaches for using digests to conduct research. The approach that you use depends on the information you have when you begin your research and what you need to find.

A. Beginning with the Descriptive Word Index

Most often you will begin your research with a fact pattern and a legal issue, but without any cases on point and without knowing which topics and key numbers may be relevant. In these situations, you will use the Descriptive Word Index to translate research terms into the topics and key numbers used by the digest to index cases relevant to your client's problem. See Table 4-3 for an outline of this process.

Table 4-3. Outline for Digest Research with the Descriptive Word Index

1. Develop a list of research terms.
2. Find the research terms in the Descriptive Word Index, which will list topics and key numbers relevant to those terms.
3. Check the pocket part to the Descriptive Word Index.
4. Review each topic-key number in the main volumes of the digest.
5. Update each topic-key number by checking the pocket parts or volume supplement, the cumulative supplementary pamphlets, and the digests contained in the reporter's most recent advance sheets.
6. Read all of the relevant cases that your research reveals.

1. Develop a List of Research Terms

Follow the TARPP or journalistic brainstorming method from Chapter 1, or use your own approach to generate a list of research terms that describe the situation you are analyzing.

2. Find the Research Terms in the Descriptive Word Index

The Descriptive Word Index is contained in several volumes at the end of the digest. When researching with this index, look up each of your research terms and write down the topic-key number for each term you find. Table 4-4 shows an excerpt from the Descriptive Word Index in *Oregon Digest 2d*. Some topics are abbreviated in the Descriptive Word Index. A list of topics and their abbreviations is included at the front of each index volume.

Table 4-4. Excerpts from the Descriptive Word Index in *Oregon Digest 2d*

ADVERSE   37 Or D 2d–50

References are to Digest Topic and Key Numbers

ADVERSE POSSESSION — Cont'd

ELEMENTS —
  Generally. **Adv Poss 13**
  Actual possession. **Adv Poss 14-27**
  Distinct and exclusive possession. **Adv Poss 34-38**
  Hostility. **Adv Poss 58-85**
  Taxes, payment of. **Adv Poss 86-95**
  Visible and notorious possession. **Adv Poss 26-33**
EXTINCTION of title in original holder. **Adv Poss 106(3)**

FENCES, see this index **Fences**
HOSTILE possession. **Adv Poss 58-85, 114(1), 115(5), 116(5)**
IMPROVEMENTS, see this index **Improvements**
LIMITATION of actions —
  As against state. **Lim of Act 11(1)**
  Discovery of fraud. **Lim of Act 100(2)**
MORTGAGED property. **Mtg 143**
  Actual adverse possession. **Adv Poss 16**
  Against infants. **Infants 24**

Source: *Oregon Digest 2d.* Reprinted with permission of West, a Thomson business.

Be sure to record both the topic and the key number. Many topics will have the same key numbers, so a number alone is not a helpful research tool.

Do not stop looking up research terms after finding just one term listed with a topic-key number. You should move to the next step only when you have a list of topics and key numbers.

If you do not find any of your terms in the Descriptive Word Index, try to brainstorm for additional research terms. If you still cannot find any terms listed in this index, consider moving to a secondary source like a legal encyclopedia or a law review article, or beginning with an annotated statutory code, and come back to digests once you have learned more about your subject.

3. Check the Pocket Part to the Descriptive Word Index

The information included in the Descriptive Word Index will be only as current as the copyright date of that digest volume. To include new topics and key numbers without reprinting an entire bound volume, the publisher prints *pocket parts*. These are additional pages that are inserted in a slot in the back cover of the bound volume. Pocket parts are printed annually and sent to everyone who subscribes to the digest. To be thorough, you must search these pocket parts for each of your research terms, and record any topics and key numbers you find. If the volume has been printed within the last year, however, it will not have a pocket part for you to check.

4. Review Each Topic-Key Number in the Main Volumes of the Digest

Take your topic-key number list to the main digest volumes and find the volume that contains one of your topics. Note that the spine of each digest volume does not list all the topics included in that volume. For example, in the current *Oregon Digest 2d*, the topic "Adverse Possession" appears in volume 1. The spine of that volume lists the topics "Abandoned and Lost Property" to "Annuities," indicating that the volume includes those topics and others that come between them alphabetically.

At the beginning of each topic you will find a list of "Subjects Included" as well as "Subjects Excluded and Covered by Other Topics." These lists will help you decide whether that topic is likely to index cases most relevant to your research. The list of excluded subjects may contain references to other relevant topics found elsewhere in the digest.

After these lists is the key number outline of the topic, under the heading "Analysis," as seen in Table 4-5. Longer topics will contain a short, summary outline and then a detailed outline. Many topics follow a general litigation organization, so that elements, defenses, pleadings, and evidence are discussed in that order.

You should take a moment to skim the Analysis outline to ensure that you found in the Descriptive Word Index all the relevant key numbers within that topic. Then turn to each of the relevant key numbers and review the case headnotes there. Write down the citation for

Table 4-5. Excerpts from *Oregon Digest 2d*
Analysis for Adverse Possession

Analysis

I. NATURE AND REQUISITES, 🔑 1-95.
  (A) ACQUISITION OF RIGHTS BY PRESCRIPTION IN GENERAL, 🔑 1-13.
  (B) ACTUAL POSSESSION, 🔑 14-27.
  (C) VISIBLE AND NOTORIOUS POSSESSION, 🔑 28-33.
  (D) DISTINCT AND EXCLUSIVE POSSESSION, 🔑 34-38.
  (E) DURATION AND CONTINUITY OF POSSESSION, 🔑 39-57.
  (F) HOSTILE CHARACTER OF POSSESSION, 🔑 58-85.
  (G) PAYMENT OF TAXES, 🔑 86-95.
II. OPERATION AND EFFECT, 🔑 96-109.
  (A) EXTENT OF POSSESSION, 🔑 96-103.
  (B) TITLE OR RIGHT ACQUIRED, 🔑 104-109.
III. PLEADING, 🔑 110, 111.
IV. EVIDENCE, 🔑 112-114.
V. TRIAL, 🔑 115-117.

Source: *Oregon Digest 2d.* Reprinted with permission of West, a Thomson business.

each case that you decide you need to read. If parallel citations are given, write down both citations so that if the volume you need from one reporter is not on the shelves you can easily find the case using the parallel cite in the other reporter. At this point, the cites that you include in your notes do not have to be complete or conform to any system of citation. They simply need to provide enough information so that you are able to find the correct case. Recording the last name of one party, the volume, reporter, and page number will often be sufficient.

The process of reviewing headnotes and recording possibly relevant case citations can be tedious. But your painstaking review of headnotes is essential. To analyze your client's situation accurately, you need to read every relevant case. Hurrying through the digest pages will allow you to end sooner, but the risk of missing crucial cases is too high.

However, you may be selective in deciding which cases to read first. Additionally, when a topic-key number contains many pages of case headnotes, or when you are working under tight deadlines, you may have to be selective in choosing the cases you are able to read. First read those cases that are binding authority in your jurisdiction. Within that subset, read the most recent cases. Some headnotes include facts, and a case with facts similar to yours should be included in your written analysis of your client's situation. Never disregard a factually similar case simply because that case reaches a result that would be bad for your client. You must either find a way to distinguish that case or find an alternative legal basis for your claim.

5. Update Each Topic-Key Number in Digests and Reporters

Again, the topics, key numbers, and case headnotes indexed in the digest are only as current as the volume's publication date. Updated information is most often provided through pocket parts. If the updated information is too thick to fit into a pocket part, the publisher will instead provide a soft-cover volume of updated material, which will be shelved next to the volume that it updates.

These supplements are in turn updated using *cumulative supplementary pamphlets*. These pamphlets contain updates for all topics, so they generally are shelved after all of the volumes in the digest. These cumulative supplements are published periodically. The cover of a cumulative supplement will indicate both its publication date and the date of the pocket parts it updates. You must check the supplement each time you do research using the digests in order to find the relevant cases that occasionally appear there.

Finally, you may find coverage after these cumulative supplements by going to a particular reporter's most recent volumes and *advance sheets*, and using the digest contained in each.[6] You may rarely find

---

6. A table at the beginning of each digest volume will indicate which reporter volumes are indexed there. Updating requires you to check the digest sections of subsequent reporters.

your topic included in the advance sheet digests for the reporter, but you will find the most current information in print there.

In summary, to be sure that you have found all the cases using your topic-key number, you should check (1) the main digest volumes, (2) either the pocket part or the volume supplement, (3) the cumulative supplementary pamphlet, and (4) the reporters and advance sheets. Of course, there will always be some window of time between publication and release of the most current information. For same day currency, you must go to an online database, such as LEXIS or Westlaw.[7]

6. Read the Relevant Cases that Your Research Reveals

You must read the relevant cases that you found in your digest search. In fact, unless you have specific instructions to provide only a list of cases that may be relevant, your primary task will be to analyze the cases and apply them to your client's situation. Review Chapter 3, Part IV on analyzing individual cases.

Reading the cases and understanding the law will be easier if you organize your approach. First, review your list of all the cases that you found. You may notice some cases appear twice because they were indexed under several topics or key numbers. Strike out the duplicates so that you will not accidentally read the same case twice. Next, organize groups of cases according to jurisdiction and then by decision date. Learning how the law developed over time in each jurisdiction will be easier if you read the cases chronologically. Finding the current rule of law will likely be easier if you begin with the most recent cases. Define your goal and organize the order in which you read the cases accordingly.

Then go to the reporters and find each case you have listed. Quickly skim the synopsis to see whether the case appears to be on point. Find each relevant headnote and turn to that part of the case. Skim that portion of the case. Only when you have skimmed the relevant parts of a case should you consider photocopying, printing, or

---

7. Note that only Westlaw allows you to continue research using West topic-key numbers.

taking notes from it. Do not waste paper, money,[8] or your time by delaying the difficult work of analyzing cases.

In addition to taking notes on individual cases, pay attention to how the cases fit together. Look for trends in the law and in the facts of the cases. Has the law remained unchanged or have new elements been introduced? Has the meaning of an important term been redefined? Have certain facts virtually guaranteed success for one party while other facts have tended to cause difficulties? Does one case summarize the current rule or do you have to synthesize a rule from several cases that each address part of the rule?

B. Beginning with a Relevant Case

If you begin your research knowing one case on point, you can take a shortcut that does not include the Descriptive Word Index. Read the case in a West reporter and identify the headnotes that are relevant to your issue. Note the topic-key number given for each relevant headnote. Other cases that use these topics and key numbers will likely be helpful to your research and analysis.

Make a list of the relevant topics and key numbers from your case, then go to the main volumes in the digest. Select a volume containing one of the topics on your list, remembering that the spine of each volume does not indicate every topic in that volume. Within that topic, find the key number given in the related headnote. Under the key number you will see all the headnotes of cases that also have been assigned that topic-key number. Repeat this step for each relevant topic-key number in your original case. Remember to update your search to find the most recent cases on point.

You may still need to use the Descriptive Word Index if the case you have at the beginning of your research contains only one topic-key number on point. In this situation, check this index to ensure that

---

8. LEXIS and Westlaw printing is included in law school fees, and thus appears to be free while you are in school. Printing is generally restricted in the real world because it is so expensive. Often print charges are added to a flat fee for unlimited use in contracts that firms have with LEXIS or Westlaw.

you have not missed a line of cases that is indexed under another topic-key number.

C. Beginning with the Topic Analysis

After you have researched a specific area of law many times, you may be very familiar with the topics under which cases in that area are indexed. If so, you can begin your research using the Analysis outline that appears at the beginning of each relevant topic. Scan the list of key number subtopics, and then review the headnotes under each key number that appears to be on point. As always, remember to check the pocket parts, supplementary pamphlets, and reporter advance sheets for more recent cases under the topics and key numbers you are searching. Even when beginning research with the topic analysis, it is a good idea to check the Descriptive Word Index at some point for additional material.

D. Words and Phrases

To learn whether a court has *defined* a term, refer to the Words and Phrases volumes at the end of the digest.[9] While a dictionary like *Black's Law Dictionary* will provide a general definition of a term, Words and Phrases will direct you to a case that defines the term for a particular jurisdiction. (See Table 4-6.) Judicial definitions are especially helpful when an important term in a statute is vague.

Note that entries in Words and Phrases refer to cases that provide judicial definitions of terms, while the entries under topics and key num-

---

9. West also produces a multi-volume set, *Words and Phrases*, containing court definitions from federal and state jurisdictions combined.

Table 4-6. Excerpt from Words & Phrases in *Oregon Digest 2d*

VISITATION

Or. 1956. "Custody" connotes, among other things, right of legal custodian to establish legal domicile for child, whereas such right does not abide with parent who enjoys only occasional right of "visitation", that is, the right to visit the child wherever it is, at certain time, or to have child visit parent for stipulated periods.—McFadden v. McFadden, 292 P.2d 795, 206 Or. 253.—Domicile 5; Parent & C 2(1).

Source: *Oregon Digest 2d*. Reprinted with permission of West, a Thomson business.

bers in the main digest volumes refer to cases that discuss, explain, and possibly define a term. The cases listed in Words and Phrases are thus a specific subset of the cases that appear under related topics in the main digest volumes.

At the end of each entry in the Words and Phrases volumes, West lists the topics and key numbers used for that case's headnotes. The example in Table 4-6 includes two topic-key numbers: "Domicile 5" and "Parent & Child 2(1)."

The information in Words and Phrases volumes is updated with pocket parts.

E. Table of Cases

The Table of Cases lists all the cases indexed in a particular digest series by both the primary plaintiff's name and also the primary defendant's name. This table is helpful when you do not know the citation to a relevant case but do know the name of one or both parties, either because a colleague recommended the case or because you used it in previous research. The Table of Cases provides the full name of the case, the citation for the case, and the relevant topics and key numbers. After consulting the Table of Cases, you could either read the case in a reporter or continue working in the digest using the topics and key numbers to find more related cases.

Alternatively, if you begin your research with a case that does not include West topics and key numbers, you can use the Table of Cases volumes to learn which West topics and key numbers are used for the case's headnotes. Note that Oregon's official reporters, *Oregon Reports* and *Oregon Reports, Court of Appeals*, now use the same topics as West reporters. However, the subtopics in Oregon's reporters are written out rather than being reduced to a key number. To search a West digest, you would need to find the case in West's *Pacific Reporter* or use the Table of Cases.

The Table of Cases is updated with pocket parts.

III. Decennial Digest

West's *Decennial Digest* indexes cases from all United States jurisdictions that are reported in West's national reporter system. This digest uses the same topic-key number system as all other West digests. The headnotes listed under each entry are arranged by jurisdiction and date. You may find the *Decennial Digest* helpful in the following circumstances:

- Your library does not contain a digest for the jurisdiction whose laws you are researching.
- There is no law on point in your jurisdiction, requiring you to search the laws of other jurisdictions for persuasive authority.

The *Decennial Digest* used to be published every ten years, hence its name, but it is now published in two parts, each part covering a five-year period. For example, the *Tenth Decennial Digest, Part 1*, covers 1986–1991, and the *Tenth Decennial Digest, Part 2*, covers 1991–1996. The most recent is the *Eleventh Decennial Digest, Part 1*, covering 1996–2001. *Decennial Digests* are updated with the *General Digest*. Until all volumes for the *Eleventh Decennial Digest, Part 2*, are completed, law libraries will retain *General Digest* volumes from 2001 forward. To search the *Decennial Digest* thoroughly, you must look in each series containing cases from the period relevant for your project. For the most recent cases, check the *General Digest* volumes.

Appendix

Table 4-7 lists several digests that may be useful in your research.

Table 4-7. Selected Digests

Oregon Digest	Cases from Oregon courts and federal courts in Oregon (and appellate review of those cases)
Pacific Digest	Cases from states included in *Pacific Reporter*
Decennial Digest	Cases from all jurisdictions included in West's national reporter system
Federal Practice Digest	Cases from United States District Courts, United States Courts of Appeals, and the United States Supreme Court (and some topical federal reporters)
United States Supreme Court Digest	Cases from the United States Supreme Court

Chapter 5

Statutes

Statutes could affect almost every legal issue you deal with in practice.[1] Often, a statute will define your client's rights or responsibilities. A statute may set penalties for failure to comply with the statutory mandate. Some statutes address new issues that are not dealt with at common law; for example, the use of electronic signatures is a new statutory area. Other statutes may codify or alter the common law, for example, making embezzlement a felony. Still other statutes are driven by policy concerns. For instance, in Oregon, the host of a party who serves alcohol to someone visibly drunk may be liable for off-premise damages caused by that person. Even when no statute affects the substance of a claim, a statute of limitations may prescribe the period during which the claim may be brought.

Table 5-1. Outline for Oregon Statutory Research

1. Generate a comprehensive list of research terms.
2. Look up these research terms in the index of *Oregon Revised Statutes* to find references to relevant statutes.
3. Locate, read, and analyze the statutes in the main volumes.
4. Refer to the Annotations volume to find citations to cases that interpret or apply the statute.
5. Read and analyze the relevant cases.

---

1. This chapter explains how to find Oregon state statutes. County and city codes are increasingly available on the state's website at www.oregon.gov, under the "Local Government" link.

I. Oregon Statutory Research

A. *Oregon Revised Statutes*

The official source for Oregon statutory law is *Oregon Revised Statutes* (ORS). It contains all Oregon statutes currently in force. ORS is published by the State of Oregon Legislative Counsel Committee in odd-numbered years (*e.g.*, 1999, 2001), matching the years during which the Oregon legislature holds its regular sessions.

After the Oregon legislature enacts statutes, those statutes are *codified*, meaning that statutes are grouped according to subject matter. ORS is divided into sixty-two *titles*, each on a particular subject. Each title is subdivided into *chapters* that address specific topics within each subject area. A complete list of all titles and chapters in ORS is included at the beginning of volume 1. See Table 5-2 for an example of chapters under one title.

Table 5-2. Chapters in Title 16, Crimes and Punishments

161. General Provisions
162. Offenses Against the State and Public Justice
163. Offenses Against Persons
164. Offenses Against Property
165. Offenses Involving Fraud or Deception
166. Offenses Against Public Order; Firearms and Other Weapons; Racketeering
167. Offenses Against Public Health, Decency and Animals
169. Local and Regional Correctional Facilities; Prisoners; Juvenile Facilities

Source: *Oregon Revised Statutes*, volume 4, page 341 (2001). Note that chapter 168, Habitual Criminals, has been repealed.

Each new statute that is enacted will be added to a title and chapter containing other statutes on the same or similar subject. The statute will be assigned a section number that places it sequentially within a chapter. Under chapter 164, Offenses Against Property, are statutes for theft, burglary, robbery, and similar crimes. ORS 164.225, for example, addresses first degree burglary. Note that the title number is not part of the citation; simply use the abbreviation ORS and the statute number.

Every state's statutes are codified in this general manner, though the names vary from state to state. Examples include *Alaska Statutes*, *Consolidated Laws of New York*, and *Michigan Compiled Laws Annotated*. A citation manual will list the name of the statutory code for each state.

B. The Research Process Using ORS

How you begin to research Oregon statutes depends on the information you have as you begin your work. Sometimes, especially early in your career, you may be told exactly which statute controls your client's situation. Your supervisor may know from experience that ORS 164.225 deals with burglary. In that case, review the spines of ORS volumes to find the one that contains the chapter for that statute; then look through that volume numerically to find the statute. Statute numbers are included on the top, outside corner of each page.

Often you will begin research knowing only the client's facts. In that situation, follow the outline given in Table 5-1 at the beginning of this chapter, which is explained below.

1. Develop a List of Research Terms

To find all the statutes that may relate to your issue, develop an expansive list of research terms. Use the journalistic approach or the TARPP method from Chapter 1, or design a brainstorming technique that works for you. Refer to Table 1-3 in Chapter 1 for a list of research terms in a particular burglary case.

2. Search the Index

Take these research terms to the two index volumes that are shelved at the end of ORS. Search for every one of your research terms. As you find the terms in the index volumes, write down any statutory references given.

Do not stop reviewing the index after finding just one statute reference; several statutes may address your issue. Note that *"et seq."* refers to the statute listed and the sections that follow it. Sometimes a research term will be included in the index but will be followed by a cross reference to another index term. Referring to that term may lead you to relevant statutes. See Table 5-3 for an example of an index section.

Table 5-3. Selected Entries for BURGLARY in the ORS Index

(Generally), 164.205 et seq.
Building, defined, 164.205
Burglar tool, defined, 164.235
Dwelling, defined, 164.205
Enter or remain unlawfully, defined, 164.205
First degree, 164.225
Insurance, coverage, 742.041

Source: *Oregon Revised Statutes*, volume 16, page B-48 (2001).

3. *Find and Read the Statutory Language*

Oregon Revised Statutes contains the text of each statute, arranged by statutory number. For each statutory citation you found in the index, select the volume of ORS that contains the chapter of your statute, and then find the statute itself.

This next step is the most important: *Read the statute very carefully.*

Too many researchers fail to take the time necessary to read the language of the statute and consider all its implications before deciding whether it is relevant to the research problem. And because few statutes are so clear that they can be understood on one reading, careful research may require you to read a statute several times before you understand its meaning and relevance.

To understand a single statute you may have to read other, related statutes. One statute may contain general provisions while another contains definitions. Yet another statute may contain exceptions to the general rule.

Table 5-4. Example Oregon Statute

164.215 Burglary in the second degree.

(1) Except as otherwise provided in ORS 164.255, a person commits the crime of burglary in the second degree if the person enters or remains unlawfully in a building with intent to commit a crime therein.

(2) Burglary in the second degree is a Class C felony.

Source: *Oregon Revised Statutes*, volume 4, page 422 (2001).

In the example in Table 5-4, the statute refers to another statute, ORS 164.255, on criminal trespass in the first degree. Additionally, under the definitions section of ORS 164.205, the term "building" includes not only the common meaning of building but also a booth, vehicle, boat, and aircraft.

To guarantee that you understand the statute, break it into elements. Using bullet points or an outline format is helpful for identifying key ideas. Connecting words and punctuation provide guidance for the relationships between the different requirements of the statute. Small words like "and" and "or" can drastically change the meaning of the statute. With "and" all statutory requirements must be present for the statute to apply, while with "or" only one part is needed. Note, too, the difference between "shall," which requires action, and "may," which is permissive. In Table 5-5, ORS 164.215 is broken into its elements.

Table 5-5. Requirements for Second Degree Burglary

- a person
    - enters or
    - remains unlawfully
- in a building
- with intent to commit a crime therein.

4. Find Cases that Interpret or Apply Statutes

It is rare to locate a relevant statute and apply it immediately to your client's facts without having first to research case law. Legislatures write statutes generally to apply to a wide array of circumstances. To be able to predict how a court may apply a statute to your client's specific facts, you must know how the courts have interpreted the statute and applied it in the past.

The last volume of ORS is entitled Annotations; it contains references to (1) cases, (2) opinions of the Oregon Attorney General, and (3) law review articles that deal with Oregon statutes. Indexed under each statutory number are lists of annotations, divided into three categories: *Notes of Decisions, Atty. Gen. Opinions,* and *Law Review Citations.* The Annotations volume is published yearly and is cumulative from 1971. Annotations to earlier authority can be located in the Compiled Annotations volume of the 1971 edition of ORS.

Listed under *Notes of Decisions* are short summaries of cases that have interpreted and applied that statute. Oregon cases are listed first, followed by federal cases. Each summary concludes with the name of the case, followed by a citation. The citation indicates which court decided the case and where it can be found. You must record the citation information accurately to enable you to find the cases in the reporters. In most instances, there is no need to record at this initial stage in your research whether the Oregon Supreme Court denied a petition for review, although that information is given in the Annotations volume.

The Annotations volume also includes references to Attorney General Opinions and law review articles. Though the list of entries in the annotations for each statute is not necessarily complete or current, the list does provide a helpful starting point for research. Conducting additional research as explained in other chapters will likely lead you to additional authority that is relevant to the statute.

C. Other Helpful Features of ORS

To make ORS more helpful to researchers, the following information is also included.

After the text of some statutes, ORS includes *source notes* in brackets. In general, these notes state when the statute was enacted, amended, or repealed. If you are working for a supervisor who does not yet know your work, you may want to include a sentence or two pointing out that a separate statute has been repealed or that a related statute exists but is not on point. In other situations, you may simply omit any reference to a statute that is no longer in force or does not apply to your facts. For statutes that have been renumbered, there is a placeholder for the old number with a cross-reference to the new number.[2] A note may also indicate when the statute became effective.[3]

ORS volume 1 reprints the Oregon Rules of Civil Procedure just after Chapter 10. These rules are important for lawyers practicing in Oregon courts. The Oregon and United States Constitutions are reprinted in volume 15. Each constitution is followed by an index to help locate relevant sections.

At the beginning of the first index volume is a "Quick Search" index. This index includes the following:

- Popular names of statutes (for example, "Adopt-a-Highway Program" and "Adult Literacy Act"),
- Terms defined by statute (for example, "adverse possession"), and
- Subjects that are frequently searched.

Reviewing this index may lead you quickly to several statutes that are on point for your research issue. For example, the entry "adverse possession" refers the researcher to ORS 105.620, where the requirements for adverse possession are found. It is a good idea to skim the

---

2. In 2001, for example, a statute regarding liability for providing alcoholic beverages to an intoxicated person was moved to ORS 471.565. Under the old number, ORS 30.950, there is a reference in brackets to the new number, and vice versa.

3. For example, a note under Oregon's statute on adverse possession, ORS 105.620, explains that this statute applies only to property claims that vested after 1990 and were filed after 1990. If those criteria are not met in your research situation, the statute does not apply.

text of statutes just before and after the ones referenced in the index. The index reference for "Adult Literacy Act" is ORS 344.770. That statute contains only the short title of the act. The operative provisions are in preceding statutes.

D. *Oregon Revised Statutes Annotated*

In some libraries, you may find a series called *Oregon Revised Statutes Annotated* (ORSA). The publisher discontinued this series in the late 1990s, meaning that the information contained there will become increasingly outdated. Because the series does have some useful annotations, however, it may be helpful in your research. For example, using the 2001 Annotations volume for ORS, two cases are listed for ORS 112.305, a statute that allows a subsequent marriage to revoke a will. Searching ORSA produced six cases for this same statute. Between ORS and ORSA, there was only one overlapping case. The researcher who used both ORS and ORSA would have found all seven cases. If the library you are using has both ORS and ORSA, you should check both during your research, but refer to ORSA for annotations only and not for the current statutory text.

ORSA is organized a bit differently than ORS. Each volume of ORSA includes not only the text of each statute, but also the annotations to cases that interpret or apply the statute. Following the statutory text, the cases are listed under the heading "Annotations." Both Oregon and federal cases are included, with the most recent cases listed first. If a statute has a large number of annotations, they may be organized into an outline to help researchers quickly find the sections containing the cases that are most on point.

E. Additional Information Online

The state maintains a very helpful website at www.leg.state.or.us. The site index provides links to an online version of *Oregon Revised Statutes*, a glossary of legislative terms, and explanations of the legislative process in Oregon.

II. Applying and Interpreting Oregon Statutes

Most often in your work, applying a statute will mean reading its words carefully, referring to related statutes, analyzing cases that involve those statutes, and applying the law to the facts of your client's situation.

In litigation, the role of an Oregon court in construing a statute is to determine the intent of the legislature in enacting the statute.[4] In the *PGE* case in 1993, the Oregon Supreme Court provided the following three-part template for statutory interpretation.[5]

In interpreting a statute, the court's task is to discern the intent of the legislature. To do that, the court examines both the text and context of the statute. That is the first level of our analysis. If, but only if, the intent of the legislature is not clear from the text and context inquiry, the court will then move to the second level, which is to consider legislative history to inform the court's inquiry into legislative intent. If, after consideration of text, context, and legislative history, the intent of the legislature remains unclear, then the court may resort to general maxims of statutory construction to aid in resolving the remaining uncertainty.

The first level of analysis consists of two steps: first reading the text of the statute, then understanding the context of the statute. In reading the text of any statute, the court follows rules of construction set by Oregon law. For example, words are given their "plain meaning,"[6]

---

4. ORS 174.020.

5. *Portland Gen. Elec. Co. v. Bureau of Labor and Indus.*, 317 Or. 606, 610–12 (1993) (excerpts only; citations omitted). Two helpful articles that analyze statutory construction in Oregon are Jack Landau, *Some Observations About Statutory Construction in Oregon*, 32 Willamette L. Rev. 1 (1996), and Steven J. Johansen, *What Does Ambiguous Mean? Making Sense of Statutory Analysis in Oregon*, 34 Willamette L. Rev. 219 (1998).

6. *PGE*, 317 Or. at 611.

and the court reads the statute exactly as written, without adding or deleting anything.[7]

The context of the statute includes other sections and subsections of the same statute as well as other related statutes. In the simple burglary example used earlier in this chapter, understanding "burglary in the second degree" in ORS 164.215 required reference to the definition of "building" in ORS 164.205. The context of a statute also includes other cases that have previously interpreted the same statute. In examining the context of the statute, the court follows additional rules of construction. For example, if a statute suggests two intents — one particular and one general — the particular intent controls.[8]

The second level of analysis refers to the legislative history of the statute, which includes the deliberations of the House and Senate as well as the committees that considered the bill that was enacted as this statute.[9] Legislative history research is covered in Chapter 6.

In the final level of the *PGE* framework, a court may follow still other rules of construction. The *PGE* court refers to these as "general maxims of statutory construction"[10] and gives two examples. ORS 174.030 expresses a preference for "natural rights" over others. From caselaw, there is a maxim that the court will try to divine legislative intent even when there is no legislative history.[11] Before following one of these or other general maxims,[12] research the cases of the court deciding your case, as some maxims have fallen out of favor.

---

7. ORS 174.010.

8. ORS 174.020(b).

9. In response to *PGE*, the legislature amended ORS 174.020 to allow parties to offer legislative history to assist courts in construing the text of statutes. While intended to strengthen the role of legislative history, the amendment allows courts to weigh the legislative history as they consider appropriate. This amendment applies to cases commenced on or after June 18, 2001.

10. *PGE*, 317 Or. at 612.

11. *Id.*

12. A classic article summarizing and commenting on numerous canons of constructions is Karl N. Llewellyn, *Remarks on the Theory of Appellate Decision and the Rules or Canons About How Statutes Are to Be Construed*, 3 Vand. L. Rev. 395 (1950).

An invaluable tool in statutory construction is the multi-volume treatise *Statutes and Statutory Construction*.[13]

III. Writing About Statutory Analysis

As you begin to understand the statute and develop your analysis, follow these guidelines in drafting your document:

- Quote the relevant portion of the statute in enough detail to provide context without overwhelming the reader.
- Omit parts of the statute that clearly do not apply to your facts.
- Paraphrase parts of the statute that are difficult for the reader to understand and not critical to your analysis. If quoting requires you to use many ellipses to indicate omissions, it may be better to paraphrase.

IV. Researching the Statutes of Other States

While the same basic process applies to statutory research in other states, some important differences deserve note. Some states' statutes are like Oregon's in containing just one number. This is true for Washington, although the statute numbers have two decimals: e.g., Wash. Rev. Code § 59.12.030. California statutes, by contrast, include both a subject title and a section number. For example, the statute of limitations for bringing suits against medical providers is located in Section 340.5 of the "Civil Procedure Code." The citation is Cal. Civ. Pro. Code § 340.5.

In many states, the legislature meets annually rather than biennially. The result is that statutes are added, deleted, and modified yearly. To prevent republishing the laws of those states yearly, publishers print updates called *pocket parts* that are designed to be inserted into a slot in the back cover of a code volume. The *Revised Code of Wash-*

---

13. The author of the recent editions is Norman J. Singer, but the work is still known as *Sutherland Statutory Construction*.

ington and *West's Annotated California Codes* are two examples of codes that use this type of updating.

Another difference between ORS and the published statutes of other states is that many other states include annotations immediately after the statute, as in ORSA, not in a separate annotations volume.

V. Federal Statutes

The official text of federal statutes is published in the *United States Code* (U.S.C.). Federal statutes are codified in U.S.C. under fifty titles. Within each title, individual statutes are assigned section numbers. To cite a federal statute, you must include both the title and the section number. The federal statute granting appellate jurisdiction to federal appellate courts is 28 U.S.C. § 1291 (2000); title 28 is devoted to courts and judicial matters, and 1291 is the section number assigned to this statute. The date of publication of that volume of U.S.C. was 2000.

U.S.C. is updated infrequently and does not include annotations, so it is of limited value in research. The sources you are more likely to use are *United States Code Annotated* (U.S.C.A.) and *United States Code Service* (U.S.C.S.). If the current text of the statute is not yet available in U.S.C., citing U.S.C.A. or U.S.C.S. is preferred over citing an online source.

Both U.S.C.A. and U.S.C.S. contain the text of federal statutes and references to related research sources. Both U.S.C.A. and U.S.C.S. include annotations that refer the researcher to cases interpreting or applying each federal statute. Some researchers feel that U.S.C.A. provides more case annotations than U.S.C.S., while U.S.C.S. provides more helpful tables and better information on court rules. For the beginning researcher, both are probably of equal value. In practice, only one is likely to be available in a private library, so use whichever one you have access to.

U.S.C.A. and U.S.C.S. are updated through pocket parts and paperback supplements. To be certain that you have the current statutory language and the most recent annotations, you must check the pocket part at the back of each volume you use, as well as additional paperback supplements found at the end of each set. When only portions of the statute have changed, the pocket part in U.S.C.A. will show the new language but will refer to the unchanged language in the hardbound volume. U.S.C.S. pocket parts are cumulative, so a modified statute will be reprinted in full. Some researchers prefer to begin with the pocket part information, focusing on the most recent statutory language and annotations, and then refer back to the bound volume.

Both annotated code publications contain information other than statutes and research annotations. For example, they provide references to federal regulations and executive orders. Both U.S.C.S. and U.S.C.A. include helpful tables, for example, tables listing statutes by their popular names. And, as explained in the next part, both contain federal court rules.

VI. Court Rules

Court rules are frequently published in statutory codifications. Court rules govern litigation practice from the filing of initial pleadings through the final appeal. Rules dictate litigation details ranging from the correct caption for pleadings to the standard for summary judgment. Court rules like the Oregon Rules of Civil Procedure and the Uniform Trial Court Rules are primary authority even when the court or legislature responsible for them has delegated rule-making power to a council, committee, or other body. Success in litigation may depend as much on compliance with these rules as with the merit of the claim.

A. Oregon Court Rules

ORS publishes Oregon's Rules of Civil Procedure, but they are available in other sources as well. A compilation of rules is sometimes referred to as a "deskbook." The following rules are among those published in *Oregon Rules of Court: State*, a deskbook for Oregon practitioners published by West:

- Oregon Rules of Civil Procedure
- Evidence Code[14]
- Oregon Rules of Appellate Procedure
- Uniform Trial Court Rules
- Rules of the Oregon Tax Court

Some rules are available online. The website of the Oregon courts, www.ojd.state.or.us, provides a "Rules" link to most of the rules listed above. In addition, the link to "Circuit Courts" on that site may lead to any Supplementary Local Rules (SLR) adopted by an Oregon trial court. As examples, the Third Judicial Circuit (where Salem is located) sets out in its SLR the hours the court is open, the requirements for being approved by the court as a mediator, and many other details. Use the index or table of contents provided with each set of rules to locate particular rules that affect your work.

Rules are written in outline form like statutes, and they should be read like statutes. Read each word carefully, refer to cross referenced rules, and scan other rules nearby to see whether they are related.

After finding a rule on point, find cases that apply the rule. Digest research can lead to cases on point for particular rules. In addition, search the Annotations volume of ORS for references to Oregon Rules of Civil Procedure. Never assume that an Oregon rule mirrors its federal counterpart, or that cases applying a federal rule will be relevant to application of an Oregon rule.

The text of some rules is accompanied by commentary by the committee charged with drafting or modifying the rules. The commentary is persuasive authority.

Be sure that you are working with the current rule. West's deskbooks are published yearly, so they are reasonably current. ORS is published every two years. Changes to court rules issued as orders of the Oregon Supreme Court are published in *Oregon Reports* advance sheets, although they will not appear in the bound volumes.

---

14. Rules 100 to 1008 are codified in chapter 40 of *Oregon Revised Statutes*.

B. Federal Court Rules

Similar rules exist on the federal level. They are published in *Oregon Rules of Court: Federal* as well as in U.S.C., U.S.C.A., and U.S.C.S. Placement of the rules varies among the statutory publications. In U.S.C. and U.S.C.A., for example, the Federal Rules of Appellate Procedure appear just after Title 28. In U.S.C.S., those rules are found at the end of all fifty titles in separate volumes devoted to rules. As at the state level, each court may have its own "local rules" with specific practices required by that court. Check the annotated codes and West deskbooks or look on the court's website to learn about local rules. The U.S. Supreme Court's rules are on its website at www.supremecourtus.gov.

Cases relevant to federal rules can be located using the annotated codes, or by referring to *Federal Practice Digest*, *Federal Rules Service* (rules of procedure), and *Federal Rules of Evidence Service*. Treatises on federal rules are covered in Chapter 9, Part II.

Chapter 6

Legislative History

This chapter covers the process by which the Oregon Legislative Assembly enacts laws. It begins with an overview of the legislative process in Oregon; through that process the statutory laws of Oregon are enacted and changed. The chapter then describes the process of *bill tracking*, monitoring the status of a current bill that may or may not ultimately be enacted. Lawyers track bills that may affect a client's interests when they are acting in an advisory role.

Next, the chapter explains how to research the *legislative history* of a statute that has already been enacted. Legislative history research is most often relevant in litigation, when you are trying to convince a court to interpret an ambiguous statute in a way that is favorable to your client's position. Understanding the legislative process is important here because that process produces documents that may help determine the legislature's intent in passing a statute, which is a key to statutory interpretation.

I. The Legislative Process

The Oregon Legislative Assembly consists of a Senate, with thirty members, and a House of Representatives, with sixty members. The Assembly meets for regular sessions every other year. The general process of enacting or amending laws in Oregon is similar to that of other states and of the United States Congress. Table 6-1 shows the basic progression of an idea from bill to statute and notes the documents that are important in legal research.

Table 6-1. How a Bill Becomes a Law

Legislative Action	Documents Produced
An idea for legislation is suggested by a citizen, group, or legislator. A legislator or legislative committee sponsors the bill, and the legislative counsel drafts the language.	The text of a **bill** is obviously important; if enacted, the bill's requirements or prohibitions may affect a client's interests. Even if a modified version is passed, comparing the original to the final version can help determine the legislature's intent.
The bill is introduced in either the House or Senate. It is read for the first time and assigned to a committee.	
The committee holds public hearings and acts to pass the bill, pass the bill with amendments, or not pass the bill.	In Oregon, the **minutes and audio tapes** of committee hearings and working sessions form the largest part of the legislative history. In addition, the **original bill file** contains a **staff analysis**, explaining the need for and goals of the legislation. A bill passed with amendments is called an **A-engrossed bill** (abbreviated A-Eng.).
If the bill is passed, it goes back to the full chamber (House or Senate) for a second and third reading. That chamber votes to pass, not pass, or refer the bill back to committee. If the bill is not passed, it dies.	**Audio tapes** of floor proceedings are available from the state archives. Votes are available in the **journals** of the House and Senate.
If the bill is passed, it goes to the second chamber for the first reading, and then it is assigned to a committee. The committee holds public hearings and acts to pass the bill, pass the bill with amendments, or not pass the bill. If the bill is not passed, it dies.	Additional legislative history, of the type described above, is produced in the second chamber. If the bill is amended for a second time, it is reprinted as a **B-engrossed bill**.

Table 6-1. How a Bill Becomes a Law, *continued.*

Legislative Action	Documents Produced
If the bill is passed in the same form as in the first chamber, it is sent to the Governor. If the bill is passed with amendments, it goes back to the first chamber for a vote on the changes. If needed, a conference committee is appointed with legislators from both chambers, who work out the differences. When the two chambers concur on the final bill, it is sent to the Governor. If the bill is not passed, it dies.	The final version of the bill that is sent to the Governor is the **enrolled bill.**
If the Governor signs the bill, it becomes law. If the Governor does not sign the bill, it becomes law without signature. If the Governor vetos the bill, a two-thirds vote in both chambers will override the veto.	Some **veto statements** of Governors are published in the journals of the House and Senate.
The enacted bill is assigned a session law number; in Oregon this is called a chapter number. This is a chronological number based on when the bill was passed in that session of the legislature.	**Session laws** are published in numerical order in *Oregon Laws.*
The law is codified, meaning that it is assigned a number that places it with other laws on similar topics.	Oregon **statutes are codified** in *Oregon Revised Statutes.*

Source: Based on *Oregon Legislative Guide* 141 (2001).

The *Oregon Legislative Guide*[1] contains an explanation of the legislative process in Oregon as well as maps of Senate and House dis-

---

1. This small guidebook is available from Legislative Publications/Distribution, 900 Court Street, N.E., Room 49, Salem, OR 97301. The telephone number is (503) 986-1180.

tricts, photographs and biographies of Senators and Representatives, contact information for members and committees, and a glossary of terms that are helpful for understanding the legislative process. For online resources for conducting legislative research, check the Oregon state legislature's website at www.leg.state.or.us and the site of the Oregon State Archives at http://arcweb.sos.state.or.us/banners/legis. htm.

II. Oregon Bill Tracking

Of the many bills that are introduced in each legislative session, some may affect the rights of a client by proposing new laws or amending existing laws. In advising a client, an attorney needs to learn of any bills on topics relevant to the client's interest and follow their progress through the process outlined above. See Table 6-2 for an outline of the process for bill tracking online.

A. Researching with a Bill Number

If you know the number of a bill that you need to track, you can do so easily on the Oregon legislature's website at no charge. The address is www.leg.state.or.us/billsset.htm. That page currently has a wealth of information; finding the exact link you need may require scrolling down a long list of links.

Under the heading "Bills" are links to recent sessions of the legislature. Click on the current session. There you will see links to the full text of bills introduced in each chamber. You can also retrieve a particular bill by clicking on "Search for Specific Measure Number."[2]

---

2. Note that the website often uses the more general term "measures" rather than the specific "bills." Measures include bills, joint resolutions, concurrent resolutions, resolutions, and memorials.

Table 6-2. Outline for Bill Tracking Online

1. Go to the legislature's website.
2. Click on "Bills."
3. Click on the current session, for example, "2003 Regular Session."
4. When you know the bill number:
   a. click on "Full Text of Measures" in either HTML or Adobe format; or
   b. alternatively, enter the bill number on the link "Search for Specific Measure Number."
5. When you do not know the bill number:
   a. click on "Statutes Affected by 2003 Measures" and review the table for relevant ORS sections;
   b. review the "Index of 2003 Legislative Measures, by Topic"; or
   c. click on "Search the Bills and Laws," and formulate a topic search.

B. Learning About Other Pending Bills

If you do not know the bill number, or if you need to learn whether there even is pending legislation that affects your work, your research requires an additional step or two. When you know a particular section of *Oregon Revised Statutes* (ORS) that affects your client, you can review a table linked to "Statutes Affected by [year] Measures." This table shows whether existing statutes would be "amended, repealed, or added to" if the legislature were to act on various bills introduced in the current session.

To learn about additional bills that are not directly tied to an existing ORS section, click on "Index of [year] Legislative Measures, by Topic." This index looks much like the index to ORS, with references to current bills on point for each topic. In addition to reviewing the index, you can also conduct a search of bills and laws by topic. A help link on the search page gives suggestions for choosing and entering search terms.[3]

---

3. LEXIS and Westlaw both provide similar material in their databases, usually identified as "Legislative Service."

If you do not have access to online sources, you can track pending legislation with the advance sheets to *Oregon Laws*. These are simply copies of the bills that have been introduced, in their original, engrossed, or enrolled form.[4] Indexes are made available periodically while the legislature is in session.

III. Oregon Legislative History Research

Legislative history research is needed when the meaning of a statute is not clear from the text or context of the statute. It is especially useful for new legislation, which has not yet been interpreted by the courts. When a statute is ambiguous, reviewing the legislative history assists in the effort to determine the legislature's intent in enacting the statute.[5] When involved in litigation where the meaning of a statute is unclear, first see whether other statutes or cases have addressed the ambiguity. If not, you will need to find the available legislative history and refer to it in your briefs to the court.

Legislative history research is the reverse of bill tracking. Bill tracking follows the legislative process forward, from the introduction of a bill to its possible enactment. In contrast, legislative history research works backwards, beginning with an enacted statute. From the statute as it is codified in ORS, you will find the session law chapter number, then the bill number, and finally the documents produced by the legislative process.[6] This part explains the sources of legislative history in Oregon and how to conduct legislative history research. While much

---

4. An "engrossed" bill is one that has been amended; the "enrolled" bill is the final version that is sent to the Governor.

5. *See* ORS 174.020 (instructing courts to "pursue the intention of the legislature if possible" in construing statutes); *see also Portland Gen. Elec. Co. v. Bureau of Labor and Indus.*, 317 Or. 606, 611-12 (1993); Steven J. Johansen, *What Does Ambiguous Mean? Making Sense of Statutory Analysis in Oregon*, 34 Willamette L. Rev. 219 (1998).

6. Most often you will be researching the history of bills that were enacted. Sometimes you may also research bills that did not become law; learning the text that was rejected earlier may provide insight into a subsequent bill that was passed.

information is available in print, microfilm, and audio tapes, as well as online, sometimes a trip to the Oregon State Archives is necessary.[7]

A. Sources of Oregon Legislative History

Much of Oregon's legislative work takes place in committees. This means that legislative history research focuses on the documents (including audio recordings) produced by the committees that considered a bill. In Oregon legislative history research, you are primarily searching for (1) minutes summarizing the proceedings of committees that considered the bill; (2) audio recordings of the actual hearings at which the bill was discussed; and (3) any exhibits that were introduced and preserved. Other sources of legislative history include the original bill file for a particular bill, audio tapes of proceedings on the floor of each chamber, and the votes recorded in the journals of the House and Senate.

Because legislative history can be confusing in the abstract, the appendix of this chapter provides examples of some of the documents described below.

1. Legislative Committee Minutes

The legislative committee minutes are not verbatim transcripts, but summaries of public hearings and committee work sessions where a bill was discussed. The minutes make note of each person who spoke, then summarize in a few lines the substance of the person's remarks. (See the chapter appendix for an example.) At the Archives building, minutes are kept in three-ring binders. Minutes from 1991 forward are available at the Oregon State Archives website at http://arcweb.sos.state.or.us. Minutes from 1926 through the mid-1990s are available in microfilm format at some university law libraries, including the University of Oregon and Lewis & Clark College, as well as at some county law libraries.

---

7. The Archives building is located in Salem; the address and contact information are available on the Archives website at http://arcweb.sos.state.or.us. The telephone number is (503) 373-0701. The e-mail address is reference.archives@state.or.us.

2. Committee Audio Tapes

Audio tapes of committee proceedings have been available since 1957.[8] These are verbatim recordings of the meetings as they occurred. They are often cited by Oregon courts in determining the legislature's intent in enacting a particular statute.

Accessing the audio recordings requires the date and time the bill was discussed by a particular committee. This information is found in the minutes. A key difficulty in using the tapes is distinguishing between speakers. Listening to the tapes while following along with the minutes may be helpful.

Tapes are available at the State Archives in Salem; copies can be obtained for a small fee. The content of a few tapes from recent sessions is available on the Archives website.

3. Exhibits

Exhibits may include proposed amendments to a bill, written testimony submitted during consideration of the bill, reports related to the bill, and even letters. These exhibits may have been submitted by legislators, by committee staff, or by experts, citizens, or organizations who appeared as witnesses. Exhibits may also include reports prepared by interim committees that met between regular sessions of the legislature.

In the Archives building, exhibits are generally stored in three-ring binders. In libraries, exhibits are available on microfilm through the mid-1990s. At that time, the state became dissatisfied with the quality of microfilm available and ceased making exhibits available in that form. Exhibits are not available on the Archives website.

---

8. Since 1981, cassettes have been used; in prior years, reel-to-reel tapes and dictation tapes were used.

4. Original Bill Files

The *original bill file* is a manila file that contains the original text of the bill as well as any engrossed or enrolled copies. The cut-and-paste version of a bill that resulted from committee action may be included, with words scratched out and inserted text taped over old text. Since some of these versions may also be included as exhibits, there is some overlap between the contents of the exhibits binders and the original bill files.

The original bill file may also contain a *staff analysis*. (See the chapter appendix for an example.) This is a summary that describes the problem the bill is intended to address, states the purpose of the bill, and explains any committee amendments. Because bills are written in outline form and often include lists of statutory language to be modified or deleted, it may be difficult to grasp the key idea by skimming the bill's text. The staff analysis is a helpful tool because it explains the bill in clear, concise language.

Additionally, the file may contain a *committee report*. This is simply a form for recording committee action, for example, recommending that the bill be passed or not. The file may also contain financial impact statements and tallies of votes on the floor of each chamber.

The original bill files are kept at the Oregon State Archives. They are not available in microfilm or on the website, although they are sometimes cited by courts.

5. Chamber Debate

Audio tapes of debate on the floor of each chamber are available, beginning in 1963 for the House and in 1973 for the Senate. They are available at the Oregon State Archives.

6. Journals

The journals of the House and Senate record the actions of each chamber when it is in session. Included in these journals are votes on bills and other measures, explanations of votes by representatives, and messages from the Governor. The journals are available in print and, in recent years, online at www.leg.state.or.us.billsset.htm.

B. Legislative Tracing

Before conducting Oregon legislative history research on your own, first see whether the material you need has already been compiled. Whenever someone contacts the State Archives to request legislative materials, the reference staff compiles a *tracing, i.e.* the staff determines which committees considered the bill and locates the minutes from when the bill was discussed, including dates and page numbers. The staff also lists or summarizes related exhibits and compiles a list of committee audio tapes. This information is saved and made available to future researchers. (See the chapter appendix for an example.)

Legislative tracings are available for selected bills from the 1930s forward, with more tracings available for more recent legislative sessions. Currently tracings are available online for selected bills from 1991 forward.

If no tracing is available, the charges for the Archives staff to prepare one are reasonable. Alternatively, you can do the research yourself. Legislative history prior to 1991 is available only in print, microfilm, and audio tapes; more recent material is available on the Archives website.

C. Print Research

To find the legislative documents and tapes that contain Oregon legislative history, follow the steps in Table 6-3.

Before beginning legislative history research, you must know the codified number of the statute you need to research. (If not, review Chapter 5 on researching Oregon statutes.) At the end of each statute in *Oregon Revised Statutes* (ORS) is a note in brackets that gives the history of the statute; this note includes a reference to the session law that was codified as this statute and its date of enactment. For example, in

Table 6-3. Outline for Legislative History Research in Oregon

1. *Oregon Revised Statutes* – Beginning with the statute number, find the session law number and date of enactment.
2. *Oregon Laws* – Look up the session law to find the bill number.
3. *Final Status Report for Legislative Measures* (prior to 1997, this series was called *Final Legislative Calendar*) – Find the committees to which the bill was assigned and the dates each committee considered the bill.
4. *Microfilm, audio tapes, exhibits, original bill files, journals* – Review the existing legislative history.
5. *Cases and secondary sources* – Cases may refer to the legislative history of a statute at issue, thus providing a shortcut in your research. Reading articles from newspapers, bar journals, law reviews, and websites can add to your understanding of the issue the legislature was concerned about, how the legislature intended to address it, and problems that may have resulted from the enacted statute.

Table 6-4 the note [1975 c.556 §§2 to 19] means that the statute was enacted by *Oregon Laws 1975*, chapter 556, sections 2 through 19.[9] The history notes in ORS provide information only as far back as 1953. If nothing appears in a history note, refer to *Prior Legislative History* to learn the derivation of the statute.[10]

EXAMPLE: You need to research the legislative history of ORS 656.005(7)(b)(B) to determine whether a delivery man suffered a "compensable injury" when he broke his tooth on a piece of candy provided by his employer. Tables 6-4 to 6-6 provide excerpts.

---

9. Do not confuse the "chapters" in session laws with the "chapters" in ORS; the session law number provides purely chronological record keeping, while the ORS chapter places the enacted law in context with other statutes on similar topics.

10. *Prior Legislative History* was published with the 1953 edition of ORS. In the situation where you find nothing in the current ORS history note and have to refer to the *Prior Legislative History* volume for the source of the statute, you will likely find that there is no legislative history documentation because virtually none was produced.

Table 6-4. Excerpt from *Oregon Revised Statutes* (2001)

656.005 Definitions.

***

(7)(b) "Compensable injury" does not include:

***

(B) Injury incurred while engaging in or performing, or as the result of engaging in or performing, any recreational or social activities primarily for the worker's personal pleasure.

***

[1975 c.556 §§2 to 19 (enacted in lieu of 656.002); 1977 c.109 §2; 1977 c.804 §1; 1979 c.839 §26; 1981 c.535 §30; 1981 c.723 §3; 1981 c.854 §2; 1983 c.740 §242; 1985 c.212 §1; 1985 c.507 §1; 1985 c.770 §1; 1987 c.373 §31; 1987 c.457 §1; 1987 c.713 §3; 1987 c.884 §25; 1989 c.762 §3; 1990 c.2 §3; 1993 c.739 §23; 1993 c.744 §18; 1995 c.93 §31; 1995 c.332 §1; 1997 c.491 §5; 2001 c.865 §1].

Session laws—the bills in the form in which they were enacted—are published in *Oregon Laws*.[11] The bills are organized by session law number, in chronological order based on the date of enactment. The bill number follows the words "An Act" after the chapter number. Senate bill numbers are preceded by "SB," and House bills are preceded by "HB."

Often a statute will be amended after it is enacted; the history note will give the session law number for subsequent amendments as well as the initial enactment. The example in Table 6-4 shows numerous amendments. Reading each of them in *Oregon Laws* would reveal that in 1987 section 3 of chapter 713 amended the definition of "compensable injury" as shown in Table 6-5.

To determine the committees to which the bill was assigned, refer to the series *Final Legislative Calendar*, called *Final Status Report for Legislative Measures* since 1997. This series is published after the leg-

---

11. *Oregon Laws* is published every two years, soon after the end of the legislative session. Advance sheets are available earlier, while the legislature is in session.

Table 6-5. Excerpt from *Oregon Laws 1987*

CHAPTER 713	
AN ACT	HB 2271

Relating to workers' compensation; creating new provisions; amending ORS 656.005; and prescribing an effective date.

Whereas it is the desire of the Legislative Assembly to provide future guidance to the appellate courts of this state with respect to the interpretation of certain of the provisions of the Workers' Compensation Law included in this Act; now, therefore,

Be It Enacted by the People of the State of Oregon:

"Compensable injury" does not include: Injury incurred while engaging in or performing, or as the result of engaging in or performing, any recreational or social activities solely for the worker's personal pleasure.

Source: *Oregon Laws 1987*, p. 1402–03, excerpt from section 3(8)(a).

islative session ends (every two years). Each volume lists in separate sections Oregon Senate and House bills from a legislative session. The bills are listed in numerical order by bill number. For each bill, the series summarizes the legislative action taken, including which committees the bill was referred to. The excerpts in Table 6-6 (on the next page) are for House Bill 2271, concerning the definition of "compensable injury," which was considered in 1987. The entries are in the House section, on pages H-55 and H-56. Each gives the date and the specific action taken.

Also included in *Final Legislative Calendar* or *Final Status Report for Legislative Measures* are lists of the members of the House and Senate for that session, committee assignments, executive appointments made, charts of which member introduced which bills, an index, and a table of sections of ORS that were amended, repealed, or added to during that session.

With a list of committees and dates, go to the microfilm to find the legislative history. The microfilm material is organized by committee, with committee names listed in alphabetical order. Under each committee, minutes are arranged by hearing date. The exhibits are contained on separate microfilms, arranged by committee and bill number.

Table 6-6. Example of *Final Legislative Calendar* Entries

HB 2271

1-15(H)	First reading. Referred to Speaker's desk.
	Referred to Labor.
3-6	Public Hearing and Work Session held.
3-25	Public Hearing and Work Session held.
3-30	Recommendation: Do pass with amendments, be printed A-Engrossed.
4-1	Second Reading.
4-2	Third reading. Carried by Shiprack. Passed.
4-3(S)	First reading. Referred to President's desk.
4-7	Referred to Labor.
4-23	Public Hearing held.
4-30	Public Hearing held.
6-8	Work Session held.
6-12	Recommendation: Do pass with amendments to the A-Eng. measure.
	Second reading.
6-15	Rules suspended. Third reading. Passed.
6-19(H)	House concurred in Senate amendments and repassed measure.
7-8	Speaker signed.
7-10(S)	President signed.
7-16(H)	Governor signed.
	(Chapter 713, 1987 Session Laws) Effective date, January 1, 1988.

Source: *Final Legislative Calendar 1987* (excerpts from pages H-55 and H-56).

D. Online Research

The Oregon State Archives website at http://arcweb.sos.state. or.us/banners/legis.htm contains much of the material explained above, but only for very recent years. Currently, legislative committee minutes are available online only for statutes enacted in 1991 or later. *Oregon Laws* are available online only since 1999. If your bill predates online resources, you must conduct your research in print.

As explained in Chapter 5 on statutory research, the text of ORS is available online. The history notes containing the session law number are the same online as in print copies of ORS. *Oregon Laws* and

Final Legislative Calendar/Final Status Report are also available online at www.leg.state.or.us/billsset.htm. For *Oregon Laws*, look under the link "Laws." For the measure's history, look under "Bills," select a session, and search for the bill under "Measure History." Only very recent years are currently available for each.

With the bill number, the committees that considered the bill, and the dates on which it was considered, go to the Archives site at http://arcweb.sos.state.or.us/banners/legis.htm and click on "Legislative Committee Minutes." Select the date the bill was enacted; indicate whether you want to view House, Senate, or joint committee minutes; select the committee to which the bill was referred; and click on the date of the hearing.

E. Researching Older History

When searching for legislative history from the past four decades, you are likely to find minutes, tapes, and exhibits. Searching for legislative history from the middle of the twentieth century is less likely to produce results. Audio taping began on a selective basis in 1957, while minutes and other legislative materials have been deposited with the State Archives since 1961.[12] Finding legislative history before the 1950s will likely require the assistance of a law librarian or the Archives staff.

IV. Initiative and Referendum in Oregon

In addition to the traditional method of enacting laws, Oregon's initiative and referendum processes allow for direct legislation by the people of Oregon.[13] The initiative process enables voters to place a measure on the election ballot by collecting a certain number of signatures and meeting other procedural requirements. The number of

---

12. The statutes requiring record-keeping are ORS 171.415 and ORS 171.420.

13. Or. Const., Art. IV, § 1.

signatures required is six percent of the votes cast for Governor in the preceding election.

Voters may also reject legislation adopted by the state legislature[14]; placing items on the ballot through this process requires signatures equal to four percent of the votes cast for Governor in the preceding election. Furthermore, Oregon voters may also recall public officials by ballot.[15]

A useful resource in understanding these processes is the *State Initiative, Referendum, and Recall Manual* provided by the Secretary of State. It is available in hard copy and may also be downloaded from www.sos.state.or.us/elections/Publications/pub.htm.[16] The manual describes the overall processes and provides step-by-step instructions and examples of required forms.

The *Oregon Blue Book*, the official state directory which is compiled and published in odd-numbered years by the Secretary of State, contains a comprehensive listing of initiatives and referenda organized by election dates, measure numbers, ballot titles, and the resulting tally of "Yes" and "No" votes. An electronic version of the *Oregon Blue Book*,[17] is also available online at http://bluebook.state.or.us as well as through www.sos.state.or.us. Materials from initiative and referendum measures are kept by the Elections Division for six years, then transferred to the State Archives.

---

14. *Id.*

15. Or. Const., Art. II, § 18.

16. Unlike the hard copy version, the current electronic version is divided into the *State Initiative and Referendum Manual* and the *Recall Manual.*

17. The first electronic version of the *Oregon Blue Book* seems to have appeared with the 1997–1998 edition. *See* "Letter[s] to Oregonians" from Phil Keisling, Secretary of State, printed in the 1997–1998 and 1999–2000 editions of the *Oregon Blue Book.*

V. Federal Legislative Research

A. Federal Bill Tracking

More Congressional material is available daily via the Internet, and using Internet sources for bill tracking is often easier than using print sources. The Library of Congress site at http://thomas.loc.gov provides bill summaries and status, committee reports, and the *Congressional Record* (which records debate in the House and Senate). The Government Printing Office site at www.access.gpo.gov contains bills, selected hearings and reports, and the *Congressional Record*. Coverage varies even within a single site, so check carefully.

B. Federal Legislative History

Researching federal legislative history involves roughly the same steps as researching Oregon's laws, though some of the terminology is different. Bills are numbered sequentially in each chamber of Congress. Generally, Senate bill numbers are preceded by an "S," and House bill numbers are preceded by "H.R." When a federal statute is enacted, it is printed as a small booklet and assigned a *public law number*. This number is in the form Pub. L. No. 101-336, where the numerals before the hyphen are the number of the Congress in which the law was enacted and the numerals after the hyphen are assigned chronologically as bills are enacted. The public law number given above is for the *Americans with Disabilities Act* (ADA), which was passed in 1990 during the 101st Congress.

The new statute is later published as a *session law* in *United States Statutes at Large*, which is the federal counterpart of *Oregon Laws*. Session laws are designated by volume and page in *Statutes at Large*, e.g. 104 Stat. 328. Finally, the new statute is assigned a *statute number* when it is codified with statutes on similar topics in the *United States Code*. The citation for the first section of the ADA is 42 U.S.C. § 12101.

As with Oregon legislative history, you must begin federal legislative history research with a statute number. If you do not know the statute number, use an annotated code to find it (as described in Chapter 5). With a statute number, you can find the session law citation and public law number, which will lead to the legislative history of the bill as it worked its way through Congress.

1. Sources of Federal Legislative History

In conducting federal legislative history research, you are looking for committee reports, materials from committee hearings, and transcripts of floor debates. Committee reports are considered the most persuasive authority. Unlike Oregon's committee reports, which are short forms, Congressional committee reports are often lengthy documents published in soft-cover format. These reports contain the committee's analysis of the bill, the reasons for enacting it, and the views of any members who disagree with those reasons. Congressional hearing materials include transcripts from the proceedings as well as documents such as prepared testimony and exhibits.

Floor debates are published in the *Congressional Record*. Be wary in relying on these debates as they may not have actually been delivered in the House or Senate; members of Congress can amend their remarks and even submit written statements that are published in transcript form as if they were spoken.

Table 6-7 compares sources for Oregon and federal legislative history.

2. Compiled Legislative History

Similar to the Oregon archivist staff compiling tracings of certain Oregon statutes, some researchers have compiled legislative history for certain federal statutes. Two reference books that compile legislative histories of major federal statutes are *Sources of Compiled Legislative Histories*[18] and *Federal Legislative Histories*.[19]

---

18. Nancy P. Johnson, *Sources of Compiled Legislative Histories: A Bibliography of Government Documents, Periodical Articles, and Books* (AALL 2000).

19. Bernard D. Reams, Jr., *Federal Legislative Histories: An Annotated Bibliography and Index to Officially Published Sources* (Greenwood Press 1994).

Table 6-7. Comparison of Sources for Oregon
and Federal Legislative History

Action	Oregon Sources	Federal Sources
Committee work	Minutes, audio tapes, and exhibits of hearings	Reports written by committees are the most persuasive form of legislative history. Transcripts of hearings and other documents may also be available.
Debate	*Journal of the Senate* *Journal of the House*	*Congressional Record* publishes the statements of Senators and House members during debate.
Session law (text of enacted statute)	*Oregon Laws*	*Statutes at Large*
Codified version	*Oregon Revised Statutes*	*United States Code* (official); *United States Code Annotated*; *United States Code Service*

3. Print Sources for Federal Legislative History

Table 6-8 contains the most common print sources for researching federal legislative history. Some sources contain a "how to use" section at the beginning; otherwise, consult a reference librarian or one of the texts noted in Appendix B of this book.

Table 6-8. Selected Sources for Federal Legislative History in Print

Source	Contents
United States Code Congressional and Administrative News (USCCAN)	Selected reprints and excerpts of committee reports; references to other reports and to the *Congressional Record*
Congressional Information Service (CIS)	Full text of bills, committee reports, and hearings on microfiche; print indexes and abstracts in bound volumes
Congressional Record	Debate from the floor of the House and Senate

4. Online Sources for Federal Legislative History

The sites noted earlier in this chapter for tracking federal legislation also provide useful information for legislative history research. The Library of Congress site at http://thomas.loc.gov provides bill summaries and status, committee reports, and the *Congressional Record*. The Government Printing Office site at www.access.gpo.gov contains bills, selected hearings and reports, as well as the *Congressional Record*.

Appendix
Examples of Oregon Legislative History

The following pages contain samples of the legislative history for the research example used in this chapter. These documents are available through the Archives Division, Oregon Secretary of State. Errors in the originals have not been corrected.

A. Staff Measure Analysis

OREGON STATE SENATE

LEGISLATIVE SESSION - 1987

STAFF MEASURE ANALYSIS

Measure: HB 2271 B-Eng.

Title: Relating to workers' compensation; creating new provisions;amending ORS 656.005, 656.210, 656.307, 656.802 and 656.807; and prescribing an effective date.

Committee: Senate Labor

Hearing Dates: 4/23, 4/30, 6/8, 6/9

Explanation prepared by: Lynn-Marie Crider

PROBLEM ADDRESSED.

There is concern that the existing statutory definitions of occupational disease and injury do not adequately address micro-trauma or mental disorder problems; that the limitation period for filing an occupational disease claim is not realistic given the long latency period of some diseases; and that disease claimants may be under-compensated because temporary total disability benefits are calculated based on the wages the employe earned at the time of the last exposure—a time which may long precede the emergence of the disease.

FUNCTION AND PURPOSE OF MEASURE AS REPORTED OUT.

HB 2271 B-Eng. excludes from compensability injuries suffered while performing recreational activities solely for the worker's personal pleasure. It redefines occupational disease to specifically include certain mental disorders and conditions that arise out of a series of traumatic events. It limits compensability of mental disorders arising out of employment to disorders recognized as such by the medical and psychological communities and by requiring that, to be compensable, 1) there must be objective conditions in the workplace capable of stressing a worker; 2) those conditions must not be conditions to which workers are generally exposed; and 3) those conditions must not be reasonable disciplinary action. Furthermore, the worker must prove that the disorder arose out of employment by "clear and convincing" evidence.

The bill creates an arbitration procedure to decide which of two employers must pay a concededly compensable claim. The procedure permits only limited appeal from the arbitrator's decision.

The bill changes the time for filing an occupational disease claim from five years after the last injurious exposure to one year from the date the worker first learns of the disease, is disabled by the disease or is advised by a doctor that the worker is suffering from the disease, whichever is later.

It requires that temporary total disability benefits in occupational disease cases be calculated based on the wages earned by the worker in the worker's last regular employment rather than based on wages earned when last exposed to the disease—causing agent.

MAJOR ISSUES DISCUSSED.

The Committee reviewed the entire measure in considerable detail but with particular emphasis on none of the sections.

EFFECT OF COMMITTEE AMENDMENTS.

The Committee amended the bill to clarify that an injury is not compensable just because it occurred while the worker was enjoying his employment-related activities but only if it occurred while the worker was engaging in activity only for his own pleasure. The Committee also amended the occupational disease language to clarify that diseases arising from repeated trauma are compensable only if the traumas occur in the course of employment. The Committee deleted language denying compensability for mental disorders suffered by management employes if the disorder was caused by public controversy or job evaluations and substituted language excluding from compensability any disorder to any employe if it arose from reasonable disciplinary or corrective action or job evaluation. The Committee further amended the bill to allow full-scale appeals of arbitration decisions where the claimant's rights are affected and to limit the circumstances in which a claimant's attorney is entitled to fees for the attorney's participation in an arbitration proceeding.

Note: This analysis is intended for information only and has not been adopted or officially endorsed by action of the committee.

Legislative History • 99

B. Minutes from Senate Committee

SENATE COMMITTEE ON LABOR

April 23, 1987   Hearing Room C
3:00 pm.   Salem, Oregon
                                                 Tapes 120—122

MEMBERS PRESENT: SEN. LARRY HILL, CHAIRMAN
                  SEN. GLENN OTTO, VICE-CHAIRMAN
                  SEN. BILL BRADBURY
                  SEN. LENN HANNON
                  SEN. C. T. "CUB" HOUCK
                  SEN. GRATTAN KERANS
                  SEN. TONY MEEKER

STAFF PRESENT: LYNN-MARIE CRIDER, ADMINISTRATOR
                  CRAIG C. KUHN, ASSISTANT

WITNESSES: REPRESENTATIVE BOB SHIPRACK, DISTRICT 23
                  REPRESENTATIVE ELDON JOHNSON, DISTRICT 51
                  GROVER SIMMONS, NORTHWEST STEEL
                    FABRICATORS ASSOCIATION
                  DENNIS OLSON, MEDFORD CHAMBER OF COMMERCE
                  RANDY LUNDBERG, CASCADE WOOD PRODUCTS
                  SCOTT PLOUSE, ATTORNEY
                  JOE GILLIAM, CONTRACTORS FOR REFORM
                  STEVE SOCOTCH, AFL-CIO
                  DR. FRANK COLISTRO, OREGON PSYCHOLOGICAL
                    ASSOCIATION
                  CHUCK PALMER, FORMER PATIENT
                  ROGER SMITH, FORMER PATIENT
                  VINCENT LARSON, PATIENT
                  DR. DAVID WORTHINGTON, PSYCHOLOGIST
                  MARY BOTKIN, AMERICAN FEDERATION OF
                    STATE, COUNTY & MUNICIPAL EMPLOYES
                  DAVE HORN, OREGON WORKERS' COMPENSATION
                    DEFENSE ATTORNEYS ASSOCIATION
                  ED NIEBERT, TEKTRONICS

006   CHAIRMAN HILL called the meeting to order at 3:13 pm.

HB 2271 PUBLIC HEARING

015   REP. BOB SHIPRACK, District 23, said this was the
      only bill that came out of the Interim Task Force on
      Occupational Disease. The real issues in the bill
      are the definitions of "occupational diseases" and
      "mental disorders" associated with an individual's
      employment. Section 2 of the bill codifies the cur-
      rent practice that the burden of proof in Workers'
      Compensation is on the worker. Section 3 codifies ex-
      isting law with the addition of lines 18-19 on page
      two of the bill. Section 4 provides new definitions
      for "occupational diseases", "mental disorders" and
      "micro-trauma". The intent is to ensure that the

100 • Oregon Legal Research

Workers' Compensation system will be used for in-
jured workers. Section 4 also defines what is not
compensable.

098   REP. SHIPRACK said categorizing jobs according to
       stress was not the House intent for the direction of
       the bill. The bill is intended to provide better de-
       finitions for the courts. All occupations have inher-
       ent stress.

132   SEN. MEEKER said the bill needed more clarification
       regarding inherent pressure. REP. SHIPRACK said the
       most stress claims in Oregon come from office employ-
       ees. The question is whether the job and not per-
       sonal matters was responsible for the "breakdown".
       This bill tightens up the stress claims system.

175   SENATOR HOUCK spoke to the use of the words "clear
       and convincing" and asked how he felt about the term
       "real and objective". REPRESENTATIVE SHIPRACK said
       they had discussed this in the House Labor commit-
       tee. When the legislature attempts to define words
       that would only have meaning to the judge or jury,
       it is very difficult to ascertain specific definitions.
       He noted that, under the bill, to get into the Work-
       ers Compensation system with a stress claim, you
       have to prove by clear and convincing evidence that
       your disability is work related; you're in the sys-
       tem and everything else must be proven by substan-
       tial evidence.

255   REPRESENTATIVE SHIPRACK noted that the last section
       of the bill repeals the statute of limitations for
       occupational disease claims and creates a new one.
       He said that many states are moving in this direc-
       tion. There is a fear that people that are going to
       contract these occupational diseases may have a long
       latency period and not be able to be compensated
       through the Workers Compensation system.

314   REPRESENTATIVE JOHNSON, District 51, concurred with
       Representative Shiprack. He also reminded the com-
       mittee that the bill passed the House 57-2 and
       passed unanimously in the House Labor committee.

330   REPRESENTATIVE SHIPRACK added that the bill also
       deals with cases where the issue is not whether the
       claim is compensable but which employer or which in-
       surer is responsible for the claim. The bill states
       that if the worker needs an attorney present, then
       whoever is assigned the claim by the arbiter pays
       for the workers attorneys fees.

C. Legislative Tracing

Listing of Legislative records in
Oregon State Archives pertaining to: HOUSE BILL 2271, 1987
(At the request of
House Task Force on
Occupatonal Disease;
re. worker compen-
sation. . . .)

HOUSE LABOR COMMITTEE MINUTES:

Mar 6: p. 1-6   (Also on Cassette 48, side A, ALL;
Cassette 49, Side A, 000-149, 181-END;
Cassette 48, Side B, ALL)
Mar 25: p. 1-7   (Also on Cassette 69, Side A & B, ALL;
Cassette 70, Side A & B, ALL;
Cassette 71, Side A, 000-061)

Exhibit file contains:
1. EXH A of 3/06: Proposed amendments submitted by
   OEA. 4 pages.
2. EXH A of 3/25: Proposed amendments submitted by
   Jerry Brown, Workers' Compensation Department.
   7 pages.
3. EXH B of 3/25: Testimony by Jim Edmunson. 2 pages.
4. EXH C of 3/25: Supreme Court decision, <u>Dethlefs v
   Hyster</u> submitted by Edmunson. 7 pages.
5. EXH D of 3/25: Supreme Court decision, <u>Castro v
   Saif</u>. 10 pages.
6. EXH E of 3/25: WC Board Hearings Division, Opinion
   and Order submitted by Evelyn Ferris. 11 pages.
7. EXH F of 3/25: Testimony by Steve Socotch, Oregon
   AFL-CIO. 9 pages.

SENATE LABOR COMMITTEE MINUTES:

Apr 23: p. 1-7   (Also on Cassette 120, Sides A & B, ALL;
Cassette 121, Sides A & B, ALL;
Cassette 122, Side A, 000-253)
Apr 30: p. 7-9   (Also on Cassette 132, Side B, 073-END;
Cassette 133, Side A, 000-417)
May 26, p. 13&14 (Also on Cassette 170, Side A, 010-042)
Jun 8: p. 1&2   (Also on Cassette 201, Side A, 034-412)
June 9: p. 1-4   (Also on Cassette 202, Side A, ALL;
   (3:00pm)   Cassette 203. Side A, ALL;
Cassette 202, Side B, 000-ca200)

Exhibit file contains:

1. EXH B of 4/23: Testimony with proposed amendments
   by Dennis Olson,the Chamber of Meford/Jackson
   County. 12 pages.
2. EXH C of 4/23: Testimony by Joe Gilliam,
   Contractors for Reform. 1 page.
3. EXH D of 4/23: Testimony by Steve Sacotch, Oregon
   AFL-CIO. 9 pages.

4. EXH E of 4/23: Dr. Frank Colistro and others letters. 6 pages.
5. EXH H of 4/30: Testimony by Colleen Hoss, League of Oregon Cities. 2 pg
6. EXH I of 4/30: Proposed amendments submitted by Diana Godwin, OPA, etc. 2 pages.
7. EXH J of 4/30: Proposed amendments submitted by Diana Godwin. 1 page.
8. EXH A of 6/08: Hand engrossed version submitted by staff. 6 pages.
9. EXH A of 6/09: Hand engrossed version submitted by staff. 6 pages.
10. EXH B of 6/09: Memo from Roger A. Luedtke, submitted by staff. 5 pages.

Compiled by: M. McQuade, Reference Archivist
15 December 1987

Chapter 7

Administrative Law

I. Administrative Law and Governmental Agencies

Administrative law is primary authority like statutes and cases. It encompasses the rules and decisions of governmental agencies. Agencies include boards, commissions, and departments that are part of the executive branch of government.[1] Chapter 182 of *Oregon Revised Statutes* (ORS) lists the agencies found in Oregon. Examples include the Department of Transportation, the Public Utility Commission, and the Board of Nursing.

Although agencies are administered by the executive branch, they are generally established by the legislature through enabling statutes. In Oregon, some agencies are created by the state constitution. For example, the State Lottery Commission was created through the initiative process that amended the Oregon Constitution.[2] The statutory or constitutional provisions that create agencies establish the powers and duties of the agencies. Each agency must work within the limits set by its enabling statute or constitutional provision.

---

1. An agency is "any state board, commission, department, or division thereof, or officer authorized by law to make rules or to issue orders, except those in the legislative and judicial branches." ORS 183.310(1).

2. *See* Or. Const., Art. XV, §4. Following passage of that amendment, the legislature enacted chapter 461 of ORS to implement it. Remember to research statutes even if an agency was created by constitutional amendment.

Administrative law is unique because agencies perform functions of all three branches of government. Agencies write rules that interpret and apply statutes in the agencies' jurisdictions; these rules are similar in form and in authority to statutes enacted by the legislature. As part of the executive branch, agencies issue licenses (such as those permitting citizens to drive) and conduct investigations to see whether laws are being followed (*e.g.*, inspecting environmental sites). Agencies also hold quasi-judicial hearings, deciding cases that involve the agency's rules or its mission (*e.g.*, to suspend a dental license or award unemployment benefits). These hearings are similar to court proceedings, but less formal.

In general, agencies function within the bounds of an Administrative Procedures Act (APA), such as Oregon's APA, found at chapter 183 of ORS. Note, however, that some agencies are exempt from portions of the Oregon APA.[3] The APA requires that the public be involved in developing agency policy and drafting rules. Agencies are encouraged "to seek public input to the maximum extent possible before giving notice of intent to adopt, amend or repeal a rule."[4] To meet this goal, agencies schedule public hearings where interested entities or individuals may make suggestions or express concerns before a rule is finally adopted or changed. The APA also sets requirements for administrative hearings to ensure that they are conducted fairly.[5]

Each of the three branches of government has some oversight of agency functions. The legislative branch generally grants agencies the power to perform their duties and provides funding for the agencies to operate. The courts may determine in contested cases whether agencies' rules are valid. The Governor is the supervisor of all state agencies, and the executive branch exercises control over some agencies by appointing their highest officials.

---

3. ORS 183.315.
4. ORS 183.025(2).
5. ORS 183.413 *et seq.*

II. Administrative Rules

Administrative agencies promulgate *rules*, similar to the legislature enacting statutes. Administrative rules are written in a format similar to statutes with outline numbering. Rules are defined by Oregon statute to include "any agency directive, standard, regulation or statement of general applicability that implements, interprets or prescribes law or policy, or describes the procedure or practice requirements of any agency."[6] Many rules supply details that the legislative branch is not able to include in statutes. Since agencies are the experts in particular legal areas, they are well suited for supplying specific details to general statutes. (See Table 7-1.) Rules also may provide guidance based on an agency's understanding of a relevant statute or determine procedural deadlines and format for agency filings.

Table 7-1. Example of Relationship Between Statutes and Rules

Oregon statute provides that an individual is disqualified from receiving unemployment compensation benefits if the individual voluntarily left work "without good cause."

An Oregon rule issued by the Employment Department enumerates the following examples of leaving work "without good cause":

(A) Leaving suitable work to seek other work;
(B) Allowing union membership to lapse;
(C) Refusing to join a bona fide labor organization when membership therein was a condition of employment; and
(D) Leaving to attend school, unless required by law.

Sources: *Oregon Revised Statutes* 657.176(2)(c); *Oregon Administrative Rules Compilation* 471-030-0038(5)(b) (excerpt).

Although rules and statutes are both primary authority, rules are subordinate to statutes. In any inconsistency between a rule and a statute, the statute wins. Moreover, a rule cannot "cure" a statute that a court has held to be unconstitutional.

---

6. ORS 183.310(8).

Administrative rules in Oregon are designated by a ten-digit number in the form 000-000-0000. The first three digits are the agency chapter number. The next three digits are a division number, which groups related rules together. The last four digits are the number assigned to a particular rule. (See Table 7-2.) Note that the agency chapter number is not related to the chapter of ORS that created the agency.

Table 7-2. Example of Oregon Administrative Rule Numbering

The rules of the Board of Massage Therapists are contained in chapter 334 of *Oregon Administrative Rules Compilation*. Rules are separated into four divisions:

Division 1: Procedural Rules
Division 10: Massage Licensing
Division 20: Sanitation, Facility, and Building Requirements
Division 30: Ethical Standards

Within division 10, rule 334-010-0005 contains rules for applying to take the exam to be licensed as a massage therapist; it requires that certain forms must be submitted with the required fee, a copy of photo identification, CPR certification, class transcripts, etc. A later rule in that division, 334-010-0012 sets out the appeal procedures for an applicant who fails the examination.

III. Researching Oregon Administrative Rules

A. Researching the Enabling Act

Analytically, the initial question is whether the agency acted within its power. If that is in doubt, your first step in researching an administrative rule is to find the statute (or the constitutional provision) that gives the agency power to act. The next step is to find cases that interpret those provisions. This research will help determine whether the agency acted within the limits of its power in the situation that affects your client. Chapters 2 and 5 explain the process of researching ORS to find constitutional provisions and statutes; the Annotations volume of ORS provides references to relevant cases. Chapters 3 and 4 explain how to find additional cases using reporters and digests. If the agency's power is clear, skip this inquiry and move directly to finding relevant rules, as explained next.

B. *Oregon Administrative Rules Compilation*

Oregon's permanent rules are published annually by the Secretary of State in *Oregon Administrative Rules Compilation* (known as OAR, not OARC). It includes the full text of rules as of November 15 of the previous year. Volume 1 contains an alphabetical list of agencies and a numerical index of chapters. OAR does not, however, contain an index for locating rules on a particular topic. When using only print sources, skim the list of agencies and determine which would be likely to make rules relevant to your client's situation. Turn to that agency's rules in OAR, and skim them to see which ones apply.

Another approach for researching OAR is to use online resources. Administrative rules are available on the state's website at http://arcweb.sos.state.or.us/banners/rules.htm. On that site, you can access rules through an alphabetical index of agencies or a numerical index of chapters.[7] More important for getting started, there is a search engine for searching the text of Oregon's rules. Alternatively, university and county law libraries provide this material at no charge on the Oregon version of Premise, a CD-ROM product from West.

After finding references to relevant rules, read the text of the rule carefully. Many techniques used for reading statutes apply equally to reading administrative rules.[8] For example, always look for a separate rule that provides definitions, be aware of cross-references, read the

---

7. Check the date on each page to learn when the text was last updated — the online version is not necessarily more current than the book version. To find out whether any changes have been made in the past few weeks, it may be necessary to call the agency itself.

8. The *PGE* framework explained in Chapter 5 applies to administrative rules as well as to statutes.

Table 7-3. Example of an Oregon Rule

833-020-0001

Application for Licensure as a Professional Counselor

(1) Application for licensure shall be made to the Board office and be on forms provided by the Board.

(2) Application for licensure shall include gender, date of birth, social security number, practice and residence addresses, similar licenses held in other states, and history of professional convictions, discipline, or litigation and be accompanied by:

(a) The non-refundable application fee;

(b) Official transcript and supporting documentation as necessary showing education requirements have been met;

(c) Documentation to prove experience requirements have been met or request for registration as an intern with a proposed plan to obtain required experience;

(d) Verification that approved examination has been passed, or state examination is being requested; and

(e) Proposed professional disclosure statement for review and approval.

Stat. Auth.: ORS 675.715 & ORS 675.785

Stats. Implemented: ORS 675.715

Hist.: LPCT 1-1990(Temp), f. & cert. ef. 3-6-90; LPCT 2-1990, f. 8-31-90, cert. ef. 9-1-90; LPCT 2-1992, f. 11-30-92, cert. ef. 12-1-92; LPCT 1-1998, f. 1-2-98, cert. ef. 1-5-98; BLPCT 2-2001, f. 9-19-01, cert. ef. 10-1-01

Source: *Oregon Administrative Rules Compilation*, volume 15, page 16 (2002).

text several times, and outline any complicated provisions. Table 7-3 provides an example of an Oregon rule.

Following the text of each rule is the history of that rule. This history can be important in determining when a rule was promulgated, amended, or renumbered. Since the legal issue you are researching will be controlled by the rules in effect when the issue arose, you need to read the history note to learn of any changes to the rule since that time. The history begins with the statutory or constitutional authority for the rule, as well as statutes being implemented by the rule. Then the history lists in chronological order any changes to the rule. An explanation of the abbreviations used in the history note is included in the introduction to each print volume of OAR and online under "Understanding an Administrative Rule's History," which is linked under "About the OARs and Bulletin."

C. *Oregon Bulletin*

Updates to Oregon rules are published monthly by the Secretary of State in the *Oregon Bulletin*. The *Bulletin* is available in print and on the state's website. The website contains the current issue of the *Bulletin*, as well as past issues from recent years.

To update a rule in print, check by rule number in the most recent OAR Revision Cumulative Index, which is published in each *Bulletin*. Skim through the list for the chapter number of the agency that oversees the industry or practice you are interested in; rules that have been affected will be listed along with the date of the *Bulletin* in which the change was published. Review the referenced *Bulletin* to learn the exact action that was taken.

Updating a rule on the state website is a bit easier. From the link to each issue of the *Bulletin*, access the OAR Revision Cumulative Index. Simply click on the chapter number of the agency. Again, rules that have been affected will be listed along with the date of the *Bulletin* in which the change was published. Remember, however, that clicking on the rule number to view the changes may open a previous issue of the *Bulletin* rather than simply moving within the issue that you started with.

In addition to providing updated text of rules, the *Bulletin* gives notice of proposed action on rules by various agencies. Agencies must announce when they intend to introduce new rules or modify existing rules. The *Bulletin* lists "Notices of Proposed Rulemaking Hearings/Notices," which allow for public comment. The *Bulletin* contains other notices as well. For example, the Department of Environmental Quality may publish notices of its proposed action on various clean-up sites around the state.

Most issues of the *Bulletin* contain a section called "Notice of Periodic Review of Rules." Following statutory mandate, each agency must review its rules every three years to minimize the impact of rules

Table 7-4. Outline for Oregon Administrative Law Research

1. Find the statutory or constitutional provision granting the agency power to act.
2. Research case law to determine whether the agency acted within that power.
3. Find the text of the relevant rule in *Oregon Administrative Rules Compilation* (OAR) for the year at issue.
4. Update the rule in the *Oregon Bulletin* to find any proposed changes.
5. Find agency and judicial decisions applying the rule in similar circumstances.

on small businesses.[9] The public is invited to offer comment as part of this review process.[10]

Executive orders also are included in the *Bulletin*. As an example, in response to the terrorist attacks of September 11, 2001, Governor John Kitzhaber issued Executive Order 01-26, administratively elevating Oregon's Office of Emergency Management to a cabinet-level department. This order appeared in the February 2002 *Bulletin*.

The *Bulletin* occasionally provides synopses of Attorney General Opinions,[11] although these opinions are not published as part of OAR. Part IV of this chapter explains these opinions and where to find them.

D. Agency Decisions

In addition to their rule-making function, agencies also act in a quasi-judicial role, adjudicating cases pertaining to agency rules or actions. There may be several levels of agency review, depending on the agency. Check with a particular agency to learn the procedure it

---

9. ORS 183.545.
10. ORS 183.550.
11. Remember that *Oregon Digest 2d* also includes cites to Attorney General Opinions.

follows. The first level may involve a reviewer or adjudicator considering the claimant's file and making a recommendation or determination. Subsequently, a hearing may be held before an Administrative Law Judge (ALJ); these proceedings may resemble short, informal trials. At the conclusion of the hearing, the ALJ may issue a final order or a proposed order. A proposed order may be reviewed by the agency, which will issue a final order.

Some agency orders are available in bound volumes; for example, the Land Use Board of Appeals (LUBA),[12] the Workers' Compensation Board, and the Bureau of Labor and Industries (BOLI) each have their own reporters. To learn of agency reporters, check the library catalog, ask a reference librarian or an attorney experienced in the area, or call the agency. Some orders may be available on an agency's website, while still others may be available only from the agency itself.

Administrative orders may be appealed to the Oregon Court of Appeals for review.[13] Oregon courts have jurisdiction to review both the validity of agency rules and final orders.[14] Conducting case research may reveal cases that address the agency rules and orders relevant to your research.

E. Other Resources

The most valuable resource in administrative law research is the agency itself. While statutes and rules are relatively easy to find, researchers should be aware that additional policies, regulations, guidelines, and decisions exist that may be difficult to access. A large part of your research should be talking to the agency's representatives to find out what material is available. For example, a handbook provided by the agency may outline the steps in filing a claim.

---

12. Opinions of LUBA, the Workers' Compensation Board, and the Attorney General are also available on the CD-ROM Premise.

13. Some orders are appealable to circuit court, the Tax Court, or an appeals board of the agency. The final order should contain information about appeals.

14. ORS 183.400 and 183.480.

A useful tool for general administrative law practice in Oregon is the Oregon Attorney General's *Administrative Law Manual and Uniform and Model Rules of Procedure Under the Administrative Procedures Act*. It is updated every two years and published by the Oregon Department of Justice. Another helpful handbook in this area is *Oregon Administrative Law* (Oregon CLE 2001). For insights on questions that are not addressed specifically by Oregon law, consider Kenneth Culp Davis & Richard J. Pierce, Jr., *Administrative Law Treatise* (4th ed. 2002 & 2003 Supp.), which is often referred to by Oregon courts.

The state's website contains more than the OAR and *Bulletin*. Agency forms, contact information, and other useful material are also available. In addition, the Oregon State Bar's website at www.osbar.org provides information and links to relevant sites. Click on "Sections," then go to the Administrative Law Section's page.

IV. Attorney General Opinions

The Attorney General is the state's lawyer. In that role, the Attorney General provides formal and informal opinions to the state that are similar to the advice of an attorney to a client.

A formal opinion responds to a specific question posed by the governor, an agency official, or a legislator. As examples, an agency director may ask whether the federal constitution preempts the state constitution in a particular matter, or a senator may ask about the impact of a statute if enacted. Some of the Attorney General's responses to these questions are published in *Opinions of the Attorney General of the State of Oregon* and cited by volume and page number. They are also available from the "Attorney General Opinions" link on the Department of Justice website at www.doj.state.or.us. Formal opinions are currently designated by a four-digit number. For example, No. 8277, dated February 13, 2001, responded to questions raised by Governor Kitzhaber about Measure 7 (requiring the government to compensate property owners when rules restrict the use and reduce the value of the property).

While formal opinions address issues of general concern, informal opinions are likely to affect only the party requesting the opinion. Some of these opinions are compiled as *Letters of Advice* and are available in libraries in bound volumes or in loose-leaf binders. Some letter opinions are also available on the web with formal opinions. Informal opinions are designated by year plus an identifying number (*e.g.*, 2003-1). An index provided by the Attorney General is available in print. It combines both formal and informal opinions, though it may be kept in a binder with informal opinions.

V. Federal Administrative Law

The federal government's agencies function much like Oregon's. Agencies such as the Civil Rights Division of the Department of Justice, the Internal Revenue Service, and the U.S. Fish and Wildlife Service are invaluable parts of the executive branch.

The federal APA is codified at 5 U.S.C. § 551 *et seq.* Like Oregon's APA, its goal is to promote uniformity, public participation, and public confidence in the fairness of the procedures used by agencies of the federal government.

A. *Code of Federal Regulations*

Federal administrative rules are called "regulations." Federal regulations are published in the *Code of Federal Regulations* (CFR), which is published by the Government Printing Office (GPO). CFR is a codification of regulations issued by federal agencies. Similar to OAR in Oregon, regulations in CFR are organized by agency and subject. The fifty titles of CFR do not necessarily correspond to the fifty titles of the *United States Code* (U.S.C.), although some topics do fall under the same title number. For instance, Title 7 in both CFR and U.S.C. pertain to agriculture, but Title 11 of U.S.C. addresses bankruptcy, while the same title in CFR deals with federal elections. See Table 7-5 for an example of a federal regulation.

Table 7-5. Example of a Federal Regulation

---

36 C.F.R. 223.2

TITLE 36 – PARKS, FORESTS, AND PUBLIC PROPERTY
CHAPTER II – FOREST SERVICE, DEPARTMENT OF AGRICULTURE
PART 223 – SALE AND DISPOSAL OF NATIONAL FOREST SYSTEM
TIMBER

Subpart A—General Provisions

Sec. 223.2 Disposal of timber for administrative use.

Trees, portions of trees, or other forest products in any amount on National Forest System lands may be disposed of for administrative use, by sale or without charge, as may be most advantageous to the United States, subject to the maximum cut fixed in accordance with established policies for management of the National Forests. Such administrative use shall be limited to the following conditions and purposes:

(a) For construction, maintenance or repair of roads, bridges, trails, telephone lines, fences, recreation areas or other improvements of value for the protection or the administration of Federal lands.

(b) For fuel in Federal camps, buildings and recreation areas.

(c) For research and demonstration projects.

(d) For use in disaster relief work conducted by public agencies.

(e) For disposal when removal is desirable to protect or enhance multiple-use values in a particular area.

Source: *Code of Federal Regulations*, volume 36, page 89 (2001).

CFR volumes are updated annually, with specific titles updated each quarter. Titles 1 through 16 are updated as of January 1[15]; Titles 17 through 27 are updated as of April 1; Titles 28 through 41 are updated as of July 1; and Titles 42 through 50 are updated as of October 1. Realize, though, that the updates may only become available months after the schedule indicates. Each year, the covers of CFR volumes are a different color, which makes it easy to tell whether a print volume has been updated. If no changes were made in a particular volume for the new year, a cover with the new color is pasted on the old volume.

---

15. The exception is Title 3, "The President," which includes executive orders. Unlike other CFR titles, it is not updated annually.

To research a topic in CFR, you may use the general index. Look up your research terms or the relevant agency's name, and then read the regulations referenced. It may be more efficient to begin your research in an annotated statutory code that contains references to related regulations for each statute. After finding a statute on point, review the annotations following the statutory language for cross references to relevant regulations; you may notice that *United States Code Service* tends to provide more references to regulations than does *United States Code Annotated*. Look up the citations given and review the regulations.

Federal regulations are available online at www.gpoaccess.gov/cfr/index.html and www.access.gpo.gov/nara/cfr/. The text there is no more current than the print versions, but searching may be preferred by those skilled in online research. The sites allow searching by key word, citation, and title.

B. *Federal Register*

New regulations and proposed changes to existing regulations are published first in *Federal Register*, the federal equivalent of *Oregon Bulletin*. The *Federal Register* is the first print source to publish regulations in their final form when they are adopted (*i.e.*, before they are codified in CFR). In addition to providing the text of regulations, the *Federal Register* also contains notices of hearings, responses to public comments on proposed regulations, and helpful tables and indexes. It is published almost every weekday, with continuous pagination throughout the year. This means that page numbers in the thousands are common. The online version of the *Federal Register* is available at www.gpoaccess.gov/fr/index.html.

C. Updating Federal Regulations

To update a federal regulation in print or on the government's website, begin with a small booklet or the database called *List of CFR Sections Affected* (LSA). As its name suggests, LSA lists all sections of CFR that have been affected by recent agency action. The LSA provides page references to *Federal Register* issues where action affecting a section of CFR is included. If the section you are researching is not listed in LSA, then it has not been changed since its annual revision. LSA is published monthly and is available online at www.access.gpo.gov/nara/lsa/aboutlsa.html.

Final updating in print and on the web requires reference to a table at the back of the *Federal Register* called "CFR Parts Affected During [the current month]." (Do not confuse this table with the "CFR Parts Affected in this [Current] Issue" located in the Contents at the beginning of each issue.) Refer to this table in each *Federal Register* for the last day of each month for all the months between the most recent monthly LSA issue and the current date. Also check the most recent issue of *Federal Register* for the present month. The table contains more general information (whether a "part" has been affected, not a "section"), but will note changes made since the most recent LSA. Online CFR Parts Affected is available at www.access.gpo.gov/nara/lsa/curlist.html.

The updating described above is similar to using pocket parts to update research in a digest. Federal regulations can also be Shepardized.

D. Decisions of Federal Agencies

Like Oregon agencies, federal agencies hold quasi-judicial hearings to decide cases that arise under the agencies' regulations. Some of these decisions are published in reporters specific to each agency, for example, *Decisions and Orders of the National Labor Relations Board* (N.L.R.B.). A list of selected agency reporters is available in an online "appendix" to the *Association of Legal Writing Directors Citation Manual*; the website is www.alwd.org/cm/.

E. Judicial Opinions

The methods of case research explained in Chapters 3 and 4 will lead to opinions in which the judiciary reviewed decisions of federal agencies. Additionally, *Shepard's Code of Federal Regulations Citations* is a useful research tool both for updating federal regulations and for finding cases relevant to regulatory research. The process of Shepardizing is described in Chapter 8.

Chapter 8

Updating with Shepard's Citators

Before using any legal authority to analyze a problem, you must know how that authority has been treated by later actions of a court, legislature, or agency. A case may have been reversed or overruled; a statute may have been amended or repealed. Pocket parts in digests and annotated codes provide access to newer law, but they do not indicate the status of older authority you may have located. Ensuring that the cases, statutes, and other authorities you rely on represent the *current* law requires an additional step; the generic term for this step is "updating," though it is often called "Shepardizing" because the first major updating tool was *Shepard's Citations*.

To update an authority, you must find every subsequent legal source that has cited your authority and determine how the subsequent source treated your authority on a particular issue. To begin, you need a list of citations to sources that refer to your authority. A *citator* like Shepard's provides that list.

This chapter focuses on updating with *Shepard's Citations* in print because it provides the conceptual framework for online updating and because using print sources in libraries is free. In practice, you may use online citators, even in an office with limited online services. *Shepard's Citations* are available on LEXIS; Westlaw provides a competing service called "KeyCite." Using these services to compile your list of citations can be easier than using print sources. Even so, updating is a time-consuming activity, primarily because of the number of sources you must read and analyze. But thorough research requires updating, and your research is not finished until this step has been completed for each authority that you use in your legal analysis.

Table 8-1. Outline for Shepardizing

1. Compile lists of citations from multiple Shepard's volumes.
2. Analyze the citations and Shepard's analytical symbols.
3. Prioritize and read the authorities included on that list.
4. Analyze the impact, if any, the authorities have on the source you are updating.

I. The Shepard's Process

To understand the process of Shepardizing an authority, you must be familiar with two basic terms and you must be able to recognize the various Shepard's books. For simplicity of explanation, we will assume that the authority you are updating is an Oregon case.[1] That case is called the *cited source*. The authorities listed in a Shepard's citator that refer to your case are called *citing sources*. Although the terminology is very similar, for each Shepard's search there is only one cited source while there may be many citing sources.

Shepard's bound volumes are easily identified by their maroon covers. These Shepard's volumes include lists of citations to authorities that mention your case during a specific time period. Later volumes supplement the original hardbound volumes, providing citations for subsequent periods. These later volumes may also be bound, maroon books, or they may be soft-cover pamphlets with gold, red, white, or blue paper covers. The color indicates the period covered. Gold covers indicate annual or semi-annual updates. Red covers indicate pamphlets with coverage over several months. White supplements, called *advance sheets*, generally cover just a few weeks. Some Shepard's series have blue *express supplements* that generally cover periods of a few weeks, too.

---

1. While this chapter uses Shepardizing a case to illustrate the process, Shepard's titles exist for statutes, constitutions, federal administrative regulations, law review articles, restatements, and many other legal authorities. KeyCite is available for cases, statutes, constitutions, federal regulations, and a number of secondary sources. Coverage between Shepard's and KeyCite is not identical.

Although each supplement is cumulative for the period indicated, complete Sheparding requires you to find lists of citations in several volumes and pamphlets to cover the time span from when your case was decided to the present. On the cover of the most recent supplement is a list called "What Your Library Should Contain." An example is given in Table 8-2. You will need to retrieve the citation lists from each volume and pamphlet noted there that may contain your source.[2] To determine whether a supplement is the most recent available, ask a librarian. If a supplement is more than one month old, there is likely a more recent supplement available for use.

Table 8-2. Excerpt from Shepard's Supplement Cover

What Your Library Should Contain

1995 Bound Volume, Cases (Parts 1 and 2)
1995 Bound Volume, Statutes
1994 Bound Volume, Case Names (Parts 1 and 2)
1995–2001 Bound Supplement, Cases, Statutes, and Case Names

Supplemented with:

— *May 2003 Annual Cumulative Supplement Vol. 96 No. 5*

DISCARD ALL OTHER ISSUES

Source: *Shepard's Oregon Citations, Annual Cumulative Supplement Vol. 96 No. 5.* Published by LexisNexis.

A. Compile Lists of Citations from Multiple Shepard's Volumes

To begin Sheparding, you will need the full citation for the case being updated. If you have just a party's name, use *Shepard's Oregon Case Names Citator* or the Table of Cases in *Oregon Digest 2d*. The example in Table 8-3 is for the case *Schoeller v. Kulawiak*, 118 Or. App. 524 (1993).

---

2. When updating a case, volumes with statutes as cited sources are not needed. Also, volumes published before the date of your case are unnecessary.

The jurisdiction or the reporter where your case was published will indicate which Shepard's title you will need for updating. Lists of citations to Oregon cases are included in *Shepard's Oregon Citations* and *Shepard's Pacific Reporter Citations*.[3] Federal cases are updated in two titles: *Shepard's United States Citations* for the United States Supreme Court, and *Shepard's Federal Citations* for the federal circuit and district courts.

Some libraries have a central location for all Shepard's titles. Other libraries shelve Shepard's volumes immediately after the authority they update. For example, *Shepard's California Reporter Citations* would be shelved at the end of *California Reporter*. If there are multiple sets of *California Reporter* in a library, only one may be accompanied by Shepard's volumes. Use the library's catalog or ask a librarian if you need help locating a particular Shepard's title.

After locating the appropriate Shepard's title for your case, gather the Shepard's hardbound and soft-cover volumes listed in "What Your Library Should Contain." Within each of these Shepard's volumes you will use (1) the name of the reporter, (2) the reporter series, (3) the reporter volume number, and (4) the first page of the case in that reporter to find the relevant cite lists.

First, find the correct *reporter name* for your case in each book or supplement. The left column in Table 8-3 is from *Shepard's Oregon Citations*, Case Edition, Part 1. Within that volume are Shepard's lists for cases published in *Oregon Reports* and for cases published in *Oregon Reports, Court of Appeals*. The excerpt in Table 8-3 is taken from pages covering *Oregon Reports, Court of Appeals*, since the *Schoeller* case citation indicates that the case was decided by the Court of Appeals.

If your reporter has been published in more than one series, find the correct *reporter series* for your case in each book or supplement. The reporter information is found on the spine of the book for hard-

---

3. Shepardizing an Oregon case in the two citators may produce slightly different results since their coverage is slightly different. Tables at the front of each Shepard's volume state which citing sources are included.

Table 8-3. Excerpts from *Shepard's Oregon Citations* for *Schoeller v. Kulawiak*, 118 Or. App. 524 (1993).

	1995 Bound Volume Case Edition, part 1 (maroon bound)	1995–2001 Bound Supplement (maroon bound)	May 2003 Annual Supplement (gold soft cover)	
	–517–	–480–	Vol. 118	← Reporter Volume
	Ailes v Portland	130OrA283	–437–	
	Meadows Inc.	131OrA⁵66	178OrA307	
	1993	139OrA⁵429	178OrA¹308	
	(848P2d138)	140OrA¹323	178OrA²308	
	s 312Ore376	145OrA107	181OrA¹421	
	s 318Ore24	169OrA538	Cir. 9	
	s 104OrA115	–497–	237F3d1088	
First page →	–524–	136OrA³373	j 237F3d1096	
Name of case →	Schoeller v	–517–	44Fed Appx	
	Kulawiak	131OrA691	[139	
Parallel cite →	1993	133OrA528	2000USDist	LEXIS citing source
	(848P2d619)	136OrA³494	[LX20229	
History case →	s 317Ore272	–524–	–488–	
	128OrA278	135OrA286	36WML549	
Treatment case		147OrA395	–497–	
	—530—	152OrA²318	f 174OrA366	
	Bergman	152OrA³318	174OrA²366	
	v Holden	152OrA⁵318	180OrA²390	
	1993	152OrA⁶318	–508–	Super-script 2 refers to headnote 2 of Schoeller
	(848P2d141)	f 163OrA352	177OrA³655	
	m 122OrA257	–530–	–530–	
		j 150OrA53	Cir. 9	
			2001USDist	
			[LX8345	

Sources: *Shepard's Oregon Citations, 1995 Bound Volume, Case Edition, Part 1, page 1548; 1995–2001 Bound Supplement, page 126; Annual Cumulative Supplement, Vol. 96 No. 5, page 164.* Published by LexisNexis.

bound volumes and also at the top of each page of both hardbound and softbound volumes. Sometimes, especially in the supplements, cites to cases in the first, second, and third reporter series will be in the same Shepard's volume; the table of contents may be helpful in determining the correct section of that volume for your reporter series. If your case is reported in the third series, be careful not to turn to the section containing the first or second series. For instance, if you are Shepardizing *Frontier Refining, Inc. v. Payne*, 23 P.3d 38 (Wyo. 2001), but you inadvertently turn to the section of Shepard's that contains the second series of *Pacific Reporter* instead of the third series, the citing sources will be for *Weiss v. Policy Holder's Life Insurance Association*, 23 P.2d 38 (Cal. Dist. App. 1933), a case from a different state published almost seventy years earlier.

Next, locate the Shepard's pages that contain case cites from the *volume* of the reporter where your case was published. Volume numbers are noted in the top corner of each page. At the point on a Shepard's page where the reporter volume changes, the new volume number is enclosed in a box.

Then, flip through the Shepard's pages until you find the *reporter page number* where your case begins. Shepard's citator pages are subdivided according to the initial page of each case in that volume of the reporter. These are noted in bold type surrounded by dashes. In the first volume that contains your case as a cited source, the name of your case will appear just under the heading containing the case's first page.

Repeat this process for each of the relevant Shepard's sources included in "What Your Library Should Contain." In the example, completed in May 2003, there were three volumes noted there: the 1995 bound case edition; the 1995–2001 bound supplement; and the gold annual supplement from May 2003.

Note that if a Shepard's volume was published before your case was decided, your case will not be found there. You will need to move to more recent Shepard's volumes and pamphlets to find the first list of citations to your case. Because the *Schoeller* case was decided in 1993, it appears for the first time in the 1995 Shepard's volume. If your case is not included in volumes covering periods after your case was decided, it means that no authorities reviewed by Shepard's cited to your case during the period covered by that Shepard's volume. This was true for the *Schoeller* case in the May 2003 supplement.

Sometimes Shepard's will list only a LEXIS database citation for a citing source.[4] This is either because, at the time the Shepard's volume or supplement was published, the citing source was so recent that it was not yet available in a print reporter or because the case will not be published in a reporter. Information at the front of a supplement explains how to learn the name of the citing source.

B. Analyze the Citations and Shepard's Symbols

You should now have several Shepard's volumes, all opened to the pages containing lists of citations to your case. This section explains the information given in those lists.

1. Parallel Citations

Any parallel citations, indicating where you can find the same case published in another reporter, will appear underneath the name of your case in the first Shepard's volume where your case appears. Parallel citations will be enclosed in parentheses. The parallel cite for the *Schoeller* case is 848 P.2d 619. If your library has the Shepard's series for the parallel reporter, the parallel cite should also be Shepardized for completeness. The cite lists in *Shepard's Oregon Citations* and *Shepard's Pacific Reporter Citations* may be slightly different for parallel citations of the same case. By reviewing both Shepard's sources, you ensure that each authority that has cited to your case is included on your cite list to be read.

2. Citing Sources and Analysis Abbreviations

After any parallel cites are all the *citing sources*, the authorities that cite your case. In the interest of space, Shepard's has devised its own abbreviation system, which makes the pages in Shepard's look like ancient hieroglyphics. While some of Shepard's abbreviations are intuitive, many are not. You may quickly surmise that OrA stands for *Oregon Reports, Court of Appeals*; you may not so easily guess that C4th

---

4. In the excerpt in Table 8-3, LEXIS cites appear in the May 2003 supplement.

is *California Supreme Court Reports, Fourth Series*, or that ChL stands for the *University of Chicago Law Review*. Other entries, like the abbreviations for *American Law Reports*, are difficult to decipher. Referring to a table of abbreviations at the beginning of the Shepard's volumes can help crack the hieroglyphic code.

a. History Sources

The first citing sources listed are *history cases*. History cases indicate what happened to your case as it proceeded through the judicial system. All of these cases concern the same parties and facts in the same litigation. Just before each history citing source is a letter indicating how the citing source is related to the cited source. In the *Schoeller* example in Table 8-3, "s 317Ore272" indicates the cite to the Oregon Supreme Court's decision to deny review of the Court of Appeals' decision.

Table 8-4. Select History Abbreviations

s (same case)	This case involves the same litigation as your case but at a different point in the proceedings (for example, the case deciding a motion to dismiss early in the litigation, followed by the case deciding a motion for summary judgment later).
r (reversed)	The citing case reversed the case you are updating.
a (affirmed)	The citing case affirmed the case you are updating.
m (modified)	The citing case modified the case you are updating, perhaps by affirming in part and reversing in part.

The abbreviations in Table 8-4 and others are explained at the beginning of each Shepard's volume.

b. Treatment Sources

The next set of citing sources are cases that cite to the case you are updating, but these cases involve different parties and different facts. In deciding these cases, the courts referred to your case. Each of these cases may be preceded by a *treatment* abbreviation, indicating how the citing source treated your case. (See Table 8-5.)

Table 8-5. Select Treatment Abbreviations

f (followed)	The citing case followed the rule in your case and cited it as precedent.
e (explained)	The citing case interpreted or clarified your case in a way that Shepard's editors found significant.
d (distinguished)	The citing case distinguished your case on either its law or its facts.
o (overruled)	The citing case overruled your case, meaning that the rule in your case is no longer controlling precedent.
j (dissenting opinion)	Your case was cited by the dissenting opinion.

Note the important difference between (1) an appellate court *reversing* a lower court's decision and (2) a later court *overruling* the law that controlled in an earlier case. In the second situation, there is no impact on the parties to the earlier case, but the law has been changed for all future cases.

Keep in mind that a treatment code might refer to a part of the case that is not relevant to your work. For example, Shepard's may indicate that a citing source has overruled the case you are updating. When you read the case, however, you may determine that the citing source overruled only a part of the case that you are not concerned with, while the part your analysis relies on is still good law. Shepard's abbreviations can help you decide where to spend the bulk of your time, but you should do your own reading and analysis of citing sources.

c. Distinguishing History and Treatment Sources

The list of citing sources is not visibly divided between history sources and treatment sources. All history cases will be preceded by a history letter; when the letters become treatment letters, or if there are no letters, the list has moved from history sources to treatment sources. If a citing source has no history or treatment letter before it, the source merely mentions your case.

There is an important difference in the page number given for history cases and treatment cases. For history cases, because the citing case will be related to the parties and litigation of your case, the entry in the Shepard's list is to the *first page* of the citing case. For treatment cases, in contrast, your case will be mentioned on one, maybe two pages of the citing case. Therefore, for treatment cases, Shepard's lists the *specific page* where your case appears. This is analogous to pinpoint pages citing to your case. For example, in the *Schoeller* citation list in the 1995 bound volume, the entry "s 317Ore272" is a history source; the first page of that case is 272. The next entry is "128OrA278," which refers to the case *Slak v. Porter*. This is a treatment case; the *Schoeller* case is cited on page 278, though the first page of the *Slak* case is 274.

Although this discussion has focused on cases as citing sources, secondary authorities may also cite to your case. They would be included with other "treatment" sources.

3. Headnote Identifiers

The headnote reference is a small superscript number that appears between the reporter abbreviation and the page number. This number relates to a specific headnote from the cited case (the case you are updating), not from the citing source. If you decide that the legal point in headnote 2 is the only part of the cited case that is relevant to your client's problem, skim the citation list to see which citing sources refer to headnote 2. When you retrieve those cases from the reporters, skim their headnotes to find the same point of law that was discussed in headnote 2 of the cited case. In various citing sources, the same legal point may be discussed in headnote number 1 or 2 or 5 or any other sequential number. Skip to that portion of the citing case, and read it carefully to determine whether it is important to your analysis.

The following example demonstrates the use of headnote identifiers in Shepardizing, which is frequently a confusing process for beginning researchers. Before Shepardizing *Schoeller*, you review the *Schoeller* case and determine that headnote 2 discusses "actual possession" of the land that is necessary for a claim of adverse possession. That is the only element you are researching. You skim the list of citing sources in the 1995–2001 list and find that the case reported at

"152OrA318" discusses the concept from headnote 2 of the *Schoeller* case. In reviewing the headnotes of the citing source, which is *Meier v. Rieger*, you will find that actual possession is discussed in headnote 1. The text of the *Meier* opinion analyzing actual possession is on page 318, but the case begins on page 312.

Again, the key is to remember that the headnote reference in the Shepard's list refers to the sequential number in the case you are updating, not in the citing source.

In analyzing Shepard's headnote symbols, be aware that the headnote numbers refer to the headnotes in a particular reporter. The headnotes may be the same for a case published both in *Oregon Reports* and in *Pacific Reporter*, but do not assume so. If the headnotes are different in the two reporters, Shepardizing for headnote 2 will produce different results. Check the relevant headnotes for a specific reporter, and be sure to Shepardize for that reporter.

C. Prioritize and Read the Citing Sources

After obtaining and analyzing the lists of citing sources, you must read every potentially relevant source in the cite list. If time allows, you should read every citing source to determine its impact on the case you are updating. Reading the citing sources in chronological order will give you a sense of how the law has developed as it was applied in various situations. If you are pressed for time, prioritize the citing sources you will read according to the following criteria:

- Quickly skim the analysis codes, and focus on any negative treatment. Look for any case that reverses, overrules, criticizes, or distinguishes your case.
- Read cases from your jurisdiction before reading cases decided elsewhere, which are only persuasive authority.
- Read cases from the highest appellate court, then the intermediate appellate courts, and finally the trial courts (if trial court cases are published) in that jurisdiction.
- Start with more recent cases rather than older cases. Note that cases are listed in chronological order, so the more recent

cases are at the end of the list in each Shepard's entry. The most recent cases are in supplements that were published in the past year.

- Choose cases cited for the headnotes that are on point for your research.

D. Analyze the Impact of Each Citing Source

As you read the citing sources, decide whether they address the legal question at issue in your client's problem. If a source analyzes only points that are not relevant to your client's situation, disregard it. If a source is on point, analyze its impact on your case: Does this new source change the rule announced in your case, either by reversing or overruling it? Or does it follow your case by simply restating the rule and applying it to a similar fact pattern? Does the new source distinguish or criticize your case? If so, why and how?

Reading the sources you found in your Shepard's search will not only help determine whether your initial case is still "good law," it may also lead you to cases in which the court's reasoning is explained more fully or to cases with facts more similar to yours.

As you expand the universe of cases that are on point for your issue, look for trends in frequency and treatment of case citations. In general, cases that have been cited frequently and followed extensively should form the basis of your analysis. A case that has been ignored by later cases may be excluded from your analysis unless the facts are very similar to yours or the reasoning is especially relevant. A line of cases that criticize or distinguish your case will have to be countered in your analysis.

II. When to Shepardize

Shepard's can be a valuable research tool at several points in the research process. Some lawyers Shepardize cases as soon as they find them. A lawyer following this method of Shepardizing knows immediately whether a case is still respected authority. At the same time, the lawyer also finds other cases and secondary sources that discuss the same points of law as the first case.

Other lawyers Shepardize cases later in the research process. In this instance, the lawyer would begin by finding cases in annotated statutes and in digests, read the cases, begin to outline an argument, and then Shepardize only the cases that will likely appear in the memorandum. This lawyer will have to Shepardize fewer cases, but may have started to develop a line of analysis that is no longer "good law." In this case, the lawyer may need to do additional research or may need to rethink the argument. Moreover, this lawyer will not be using Shepard's as a research tool for finding additional cases and secondary sources.

Regardless of when you decided to Shepardize, whether early or late in the research process, the end result should be that you find all current and relevant authorities for your legal issues. You should continue Shepardizing cases and other authorities until the moment your final document is submitted. Shepard's is continually publishing updated information. The case you Shepardized two weeks ago could have been overruled yesterday. For last minute information, call (800) 899-6000 for Shepard's Daily Update or check online.

III. Updating Other Authorities

While this chapter has focused on Shepardizing a case, remember that many authorities can be Shepardized. *Shepard's Oregon Citations* also includes citations for statutes, constitutional provisions, opinions of the attorney general, court rules, and jury instructions. In addition, Shepard's series exist for federal cases, statutes, and regulations as well as for a number of secondary sources. Use your library's catalog to learn whether you have Shepard's for these authorities.

IV. Online Updating

An important question to ask in updating is whether you have access to online services. Either the LEXIS version of Shepard's or Westlaw's KeyCite will provide more current updating information than is available in print sources.[5] The online services are initially much easier to use than print sources because gathering cumulative lists of citing sources online with LEXIS or Westlaw is quicker than compiling the lists with Shepard's print volumes.[6] Electronic updating still takes considerable time because most of your effort will still go to reading the cases in the citation list.

V. Ethics

Courts expect lawyers to Shepardize to ensure that their arguments are supported and to present the current state of the law to the courts. The Oregon Court of Appeals has noted that "failure to 'Shepardize' a key case" is "not excusable." *McCarthy v. Oregon Freeze Dry, Inc.*, 158 Or. App. 654, 656 (1999).

Failing to cite current law or to disclose adverse authority may result in sanctions, malpractice suits, public embarrassment, and damage to your reputation. In one instance, a judge ordered a major law firm to copy for each of its partners and associates an opinion chastising the firm for failing to cite a case adverse to the client's argument. *Golden Eagle Distribg. Corp. v. Burroughs Corp.*, 103 F.R.D. 124, 129 (N.D. Cal. 1984) ("For counsel to have been unaware of those cases means that they did not Shepardize their principal authority...."). In another case, an attorney was suspended from practice for dishon-

---

5. Shepard's CD-ROM product provides some of the benefits of online updating though it is not as current.

6. One complication is that Shepard's is a LEXIS product, and LEXIS cases online have different headnotes than the headnotes in West reporters. Custom Shepardizing may allow you to access West headnotes on LEXIS, but take care.

esty to his client, misuse of client funds, and failure to file the client's claim within the limitations period. In reviewing the facts of the case, the court noted that the attorney "had not Shepardized the cases he relied on regarding the statute of limitations." *In re Tway*, 919 P.2d 323, 325 (Idaho 1996).

Chapter 9

Secondary Sources
and Practice Aids

Other lawyers have previously researched and analyzed many of the issues that you will face in law practice. Many have published their work in legal encyclopedias, treatises, law review articles, practice handbooks, and other secondary sources. These sources are "secondary" because they are written by law professors, practicing attorneys, legal editors, and even law students. In contrast, "primary" authority is written by legislatures, courts, and administrative agencies.

Lawyers use secondary sources to learn about the law and to find references to relevant primary authority. Often, beginning a new research project in a secondary source will be more effective than beginning immediately to search for statutes or cases on point. By locating and understanding secondary sources on point, you can more easily comprehend the analysis of your problem and more quickly find pertinent primary authority. The text of a secondary source will likely explain terminology and concepts unfamiliar to you. This will make it possible for you to develop a more effective list of research terms. It will also help you understand the cases and statutes when you read them. Secondary sources often provide a shortcut to researching primary authority by including numerous references to cases, statutes, and rules.

This chapter introduces legal encyclopedias, treatises and other books, legal periodicals (including law reviews and bar journals), *American Law Reports* (a hybrid commentary-reporter), continuing legal education (CLE) publications, forms, topical "mini-libraries," restatements, uniform laws and model codes, ethical rules, and jury instructions.[1] The chapter concludes with a discussion of when and how to use secondary sources in your research.

Despite the title of this chapter, some primary authority is covered here. *American Law Reports* volumes include the full text of judicial opinions in addition to commentary. Mini-libraries are valuable because they include under one title statutes, administrative regulations, annotations to judicial and administrative decisions, and commentary.

The process for researching secondary sources varies depending on the source. A general outline is provided in Table 9-1.

Table 9-1. Outline for Researching Secondary Sources

1. Generate a list of research terms.
2. Search your library's catalog for the location of relevant secondary sources.
3. Search the index of a secondary source.
4. Find the relevant portion of the main volumes. Reading the commentary will assist your comprehension of the legal issues. Within the commentary, often in footnotes, you will find references to primary authority.
5. Update the secondary source, if possible.
6. Read primary authority.

I. Legal Encyclopedias

Like other encyclopedias you may be familiar with, legal encyclopedias provide general information on a wide variety of legal subjects. Legal encyclopedias are organized by subject matter under *topics*, which are presented alphabetically in bound volumes. The two national legal encyclopedias are *Corpus Juris Secundum* (C.J.S.) and *American Jurisprudence, Second Edition* (Am. Jur. 2d). Table 9-2 contains a short excerpt from C.J.S. Some larger states have their own en-

---

1. This chapter cannot include an exhaustive list of all Oregon practice materials. For references to magazines, newsletters, and materials in specific areas of law, see Karen S. Beck, *Oregon Practice Materials: A Selective Annotated Bibliography,* 88 Law Libr. J. 288 (1996).

cyclopedias, including *California Jurisprudence, Third Edition* and *Florida Jurisprudence 2d.* Oregon does not have its own encyclopedia.

To use an encyclopedia, review its softbound index volumes for your research terms. The references will include both an abbreviated word or phrase—the topic—and a section number.[2] The encyclopedia's topic abbreviations are explained in tables in the front of the index volumes. Select the bound volume containing a relevant topic. The spine of each volume includes the range of topics included in that volume.

Next, skim the material at the beginning of that topic for an overview and general information. Then turn to the particular section number given in the index and read the text there. The text of most encyclopedia entries is cursory because the goal of the writers is to summarize the law. Encyclopedia entries will identify any variations that exist between different jurisdictions, but they do not attempt to resolve differences or recommend improvements in the law. Pocket parts—additional pages inserted in the back of a volume—sometimes provide updated commentary.

One potentially helpful feature of an encyclopedia is the list of footnotes accompanying the text. If a footnote refers to recent, primary authority from your jurisdiction, you will have made a great step forward in your research. However, because the footnotes in C.J.S. and Am. Jur. 2d cite to authorities from all American jurisdictions and tend to be dated, the chance of finding a reference to a recent, relevant case is limited. The encyclopedia's pocket parts may offer better prospects for researching primary authority.[3]

An encyclopedia may also contain cross-references to other sources. For example, C.J.S. includes cross-references to relevant top-

---

2. Do not confuse these topics and section numbers with the West digest system of topics and key numbers discussed in Chapter 4.

3. Additionally, you could Shepardize an older relevant case to find more recent authority on point, or use the topic-key numbers given in a case from another jurisdiction to jump-start your research in your jurisdiction.

ics and key numbers in West's digests. Similarly, Am. Jur. 2d cross-references *American Law Reports,* discussed later in this chapter.

Table 9-2. Excerpt from C.J.S. Topic "Contracts"

17 C.J.S. **Contracts § 96**

§ 96. Withholding competition; covenants not to compete

Withholding of competition, when not contrary to public policy, is valuable consideration; an initial offer of employment may constitute consideration for the employee's promise not to compete with his or her employer and, in some jurisdictions, the continuation of employment is sufficient to support a postemployment covenant not to compete entered into after the onset of the employment relationship.

Library References
Contracts ⚷ 54(2), 65(2).

The withholding of competition, when not contrary to public policy, is valuable consideration.[80] Prior to analyzing the reasonableness of a covenant not to compete, a court ordinarily must find that the covenant is ancillary to a valid contract and must determine whether there is adequate consideration to support the covenant.[81]

Simultaneous execution insufficient

80. U.S.—National Homes Corp. v. Lester Industries, Inc., 404 F.2d 225 (4th Cir. 1968); In re Adams Laboratories, Inc., 3 B.R. 495 (Bankr. E.D. Va. 1980).
N.M.—Taylor v. Lovelace Clinic, 78 N.M. 460, 432 P.2d 816 (1967).
N.C.—Seaboard Industries, Inc. v. Blair, 10 N.C. App. 323, 178 S.E.2d 781 (1971).
Tenn.—Ramsey v. Mutual Supply Co., 58 Tenn. App. 164, 427 S.W.2d 849 (1968).
W. Va.—PEMCO Corp. v. Rose, 163 W. Va. 420, 257 S.E.2d 885 (1979).
Sufficiency of consideration for covenants in partial restraint of trade, such as agreements to refrain from competition, see § 259.

81. Ill.—Abel v. Fox, 274 Ill. App. 3d 811, 211 Ill. Dec. 129, 654 N.E.2d 591, 11 I.E.R. Cas. (BNA) 533 (4th Dist. 1995).

Source: 17 *Corpus Juris Secundum* Contracts § 96, page 563 (1999). Reprinted with permission of West, a Thomson business.

II. Treatises and Other Books

A book on a legal topic can provide a deeper discussion and more relevant references than might be found in an encyclopedia entry. Legal texts include treatises, hornbooks, and *Nutshells*. All of these books share the purpose of covering a particular legal subject, such as contracts or civil procedure. They are distinguished mainly by their level of coverage. Treatises are generally considered to be more comprehensive statements on a subject than hornbooks, which offer a slightly more summarized view. *Nutshells* are a series of books published by West that offer an even more condensed explanation of law than hornbooks. Accordingly, an attorney may use a treatise to become familiar with a new area of legal practice, while a law student might typically turn to a hornbook or *Nutshell* to prepare for class, or later to gain a better understanding of a class lecture.

Treatises, hornbooks, and *Nutshells* can be located by using a library's catalog and searching for the general subject matter of your research project. After finding one book on point, scan the other titles shelved around it for additional resources.

To use a treatise or other book, begin with either the table of contents or the index. In multi-volume treatises, the index is often in the last volume of the series. Locate your research terms and record the references given. A reference will be to a page number, section number, or paragraph number, depending on the publisher. The table of contents or index should indicate which type of number is referenced. Turn to that part of the book, read the text, and note any pertinent primary authority cited in the footnotes.

Some treatises are so well known and widely respected that a colleague or supervisor may suggest that you begin research with a particular title. Examples include *Prosser & Keeton on the Law of Torts*; Kirkpatrick's *Oregon Evidence*; Wright & Miller's *Federal Practice and Procedure*; and Moore's *Federal Practice*. The first two examples cover the law of torts and Oregon evidence, respectively, in one volume. The last two examples are multi-volume treatises. Table 9-3 provides a sample page from a well known treatise.

Table 9-3. Excerpt from Wright & Miller's
Federal Practice and Procedure

A. GENERAL FEDERAL QUESTION
JURISDICTION

---

§ 3561. Federal Question Jurisdiction—In General

The Constitution provides that federal courts may be given jurisdiction over "Cases, in Law and Equity, arising under this Constitution, the Laws of the United States, and Treaties made, or which shall be made, under their authority."[1] Cases that fall under this head of jurisdiction usually are spoken of as involving a "federal question."[2]

Although this federal question jurisdiction was one of the principal reasons that the Constitution authorized Congress to create a system of inferior federal

1. Constitution

U.S. Const., Art. III, § 2.

2. "Federal question"

E.g., Thurston Motor Lines, Inc. v. Jordan K. Rand, Ltd., 1983, 103 S.Ct. 1343, 1344, 460 U.S. 533, ___, 75 L.Ed.2d 260.

E.g., Steffel v. Thompson, 1974, 94 S.Ct. 1209, 1218, 415 U.S. 452, 464, 39 L.Ed.2d 505.

Oneida Indian Nation v. County of Oneida, 1974, 94 S.Ct. 772, 776, 785, 414 U.S. 661, 39 L.Ed.2d 73.

American Law Institute, Study of Division of Jurisdiction between State and Federal Courts, Official Draft, 1969, p. 162.

See also § 3562 n. 4.

Compare, however, London, "Federal Question" Jurisdiction—A Snare and a Delusion, 1959, 57 Mich.L. Rev. 835.

Source: Charles A. Wright & Arthur R. Miller, *Federal Practice and Procedure* vol. 13B, 2 (1984). Reprinted with permission of West, a Thomson business.

Treatises are updated in a variety of ways. Bound volumes like *Prosser & Keeton on the Law of Torts* and Wright & Miller's *Federal Practice and Procedure* are updated with pocket parts. Kirkpatrick's *Oregon Evidence* is updated with pocket parts, then with subsequent editions. Moore's *Federal Practice* is published in loose-leaf binders, which are updated by replacing outdated pages throughout the binder with current material. Each page is dated to show when it was last updated. Also, new pages at the beginning of loose-leaf binders are often in different colors to draw the reader's attention. *Nutshells* are published in subsequent editions much more frequently than are treatises or hornbooks.

The authoritative value of a book depends largely on the reputation of the author. Laird Kirkpatrick is a widely recognized expert on Oregon evidence, and his treatise is so respected that it is cited by courts. In contrast, a *Nutshell* on evidence is designed as a study guide for students or a quick overview for practitioners, and it would not be considered authoritative.

III. Legal Periodicals

A. Law Reviews and Journals

Law reviews and law journals publish scholarly articles written by law professors, judges, practitioners, and students. Each article explores in great detail a specific legal issue. Freed from the constraints of representing a client's interests or deciding a particular case, an author is able to explore whether the laws currently in force are the best legal rules and to propose changes.

Reading articles published in law reviews and journals can provide a thorough understanding of current law because the authors often explain the existing law before making their recommendations. These articles may also identify weaknesses or new trends in the law that might address your client's situation. The many footnotes in law review and law journal articles can provide excellent summaries of relevant research. Articles written by students are called "Notes" or "Comments." Although not as authoritative as articles written by rec-

Table 9-4. Law Reviews and Journals
Published by Oregon Law Schools

Animal Law Review - Lewis & Clark Law School

Environmental Law - Lewis & Clark Law School

International Legal Perspectives - Lewis & Clark Law School

Journal of Small and Emerging Business Law - Lewis & Clark Law School

Journal of Environmental Law and Litigation - University of Oregon School of Law

Oregon Law Review - University of Oregon School of Law

Oregon Review of International Law - University of Oregon School of Law

Willamette Journal of International Law and Dispute Resolution - Willamette University College of Law

Willamette Law Review - Willamette University College of Law

---

ognized experts, student articles can provide clear and careful analysis and their footnotes are valuable research tools.

Shorter law review pieces, generally written by students, simply summarize a recent case that the publication's editors consider important. These are called "Case Notes" or "Recent Developments." They notify readers of important developments in the law but do not analyze or critique the case in any depth. They are often not helpful beyond offering a short summary of the case and the court's analysis.

Law reviews and law journals are generally published by law students who were selected according to grades or through a competition for membership on the editorial board. Most law reviews have general audiences and cover a broad range of topics. Examples include *Oregon Law Review, Yale Law Journal,* and *Stetson Law Review.* A growing number of other law journals focus on a specific area of law, for example, the *Journal of Environmental Law and Litigation* and *Columbia Journal of Transnational Law.* Table 9-4 lists law reviews and journals published by Oregon law schools. Still other law journals are "peer edited," meaning that law professors select and edit the articles to be published. Examples of this type of law journal are the *Journal of Legal Education* and *Legal Writing: The Journal of the Legal Writing Institute.*

Periodicals are published first in soft-cover booklets. Later, several issues will be bound into a single volume. Articles are located by volume number, the name of the journal, and the first page of the article.

Law review and law journal articles are not updated in the usual sense, but you can find out whether an article has been cited favorably or unfavorably by using *Shepard's Law Review Citations* or an online updating service.

B. Bar Journals

Each state's bar journal contains articles of particular interest to attorneys practicing in that state. The American Bar Association publishes the *ABA Journal*, which has articles of general interest to attorneys across the nation.

Articles in bar journals are often shorter than the articles published in law reviews and do not have the extensive footnotes found in law review articles. Moreover, the bar journal articles have a practitioner's focus. For example, the *Oregon State Bar Journal* contains frequent articles on trends in law practice and firm management as well as articles analyzing recent court decisions.

C. Locating Articles

A popular index of legal periodicals is the *Current Law Index* (CLI). Although not published until 1980, this index offers detailed subject indexing. The CLI is available in a CD-ROM version called LegalTrac, which is available at computer terminals in many libraries. Because it is cumulative, eliminating the need to check multiple volumes, it is much easier to use than print sources. It is updated monthly.

For a subscription, HeinOnline offers full-text searching of a large number of journal articles. The focus of the service was originally pre-1980 material, but the collection is expanding. A number of law school libraries subscribe to this service, making it free to their students; the website is www.heinonline.org.

An important print index for legal periodicals is the *Index to Legal Periodicals and Books* (ILPB), previously called the *Index to Legal Periodicals*. This index is especially useful in finding older articles because its coverage extends back to the early 1900s. ILPB indexes articles by both subject and author in a single alphabetical list. Thus, articles under the subject heading "Education" may be followed by an article under the author heading "Edwards, Linda Holdeman." ILPB volumes are published yearly. They are not cumulative, but are updated with soft-cover pamphlets. Monthly pamphlets are replaced periodically by quarterly pamphlets. These quarterly pamphlets stay on the shelves until the annual bound volume becomes available, sometimes several years later. The ILPB is available online from the HW Wilson Company at www.hwwilson.com. That site contains indexes for non-legal periodicals, too.

IV. *American Law Reports*

American Law Reports (A.L.R.) is a hybrid resource, offering both commentary on certain legal subjects and the full text of published cases on those subjects. The commentary articles are called *annotations*. They tend to focus on very narrow topics, take a practitioner's view, and provide a survey of the law in different jurisdictions. Thus, an annotation on the exact topic of your research is likely to be extremely helpful. Annotations are written by lawyers who are knowledgeable, but are not necessarily recognized experts. Each annotation is accompanied by a full-length case. This case may contain different editorial enhancements from those in a reporter, but the court's opinion will be exactly the same.

EXAMPLE: In 1986, Congress passed the *Emergency Medical Treatment and Active Labor Act*, 42 U.S.C. § 1395dd (EMTALA). A.L.R. reports a leading EMTALA case, *Thornton v. Southwest Detroit Hospital*, at 104 A.L.R. Fed. 157. The official cite for that case is 895 F.2d 1131. Following the *Thornton* case is an annotation, *Construction and Application of Emergency Medical Treatment and Active Labor Act (42 U.S.C.A. § 1395dd)*, written by a lawyer named Melissa K. Stull. Among some of the topics discussed in this annotation are the reasons Congress enacted EMTALA, the effect of related statutes, the liability imposed on hospitals, and available remedies.

There are several A.L.R. series. Early series contained both state and federal subjects. Currently, federal subjects are included in *A.L.R. Federal*. State subjects are discussed in numbered series: A.L.R.3d through A.L.R.5th. To locate an A.L.R. series in your library, search the library catalog for *American Law Reports*. Be aware that sometimes the various A.L.R. series are not shelved near one another.

A.L.R. has several tools for finding helpful material. The *A.L.R. Digest* includes references to annotations, practice aids, and cases published in full in A.L.R. in the 3d, 4th, 5th, and Fed series. The *A.L.R. Index* includes references to annotations in the 2d, 3d, 4th, 5th, and Fed series. The *A.L.R. Digest* and the *A.L.R. Index* are multi-volume references. In addition, the one-volume *A.L.R. Fed Quick Index* is available for finding annotations in the A.L.R. Fed series. A similar quick index is available in one volume for A.L.R. 3d, 4th, and 5th.

A.L.R. annotations are updated with pocket parts. You should also check the Annotation History Table in the index volumes to see whether an annotation has been supplemented or superseded by another annotation, rather than just updated in pocket parts.

V. Continuing Legal Education Publications and Practice Guides

Attorneys in Oregon are required to attend continuing legal education (CLE) courses periodically to maintain their membership in the state's bar. These courses often present very practical information. Topics range from ethical issues in business law to building a personal injury practice. A CLE course may be aimed at new lawyers just learning the fundamentals of practice; however, many CLE courses are intended to offer new insights on cutting-edge legal issues. A CLE course may be led by a practitioner, judge, or law professor. Frequently, the person leading the course prepares handouts that include sample forms, sample documents, and explanations. These handouts are compiled by the bar association, bound, and published without being typeset.

In addition to binding and publishing CLE handouts, bar associations also publish more comprehensive practice guides for particular areas of law. Unlike handouts compiled from CLE courses, these guides are usually typeset and indexed. Some fill multi-volume binders.

The Oregon State Bar publishes many of these CLE handbooks and practice guides. Some of the largest publishers of similar materials are the Practising Law Institute (PLI), the American Law Institute (ALI), and the American Bar Association (ABA). CLE material is located by searching the library catalog by topic or by author, using the names of the more common CLE publishers as search terms.

Some CLE handbooks and practice guides are published in loose-leaf binders, and are updated by replacing outdated pages. Others may be republished in full, or more recent CLE sessions may be held. Always be sure that you are using the most current material available by checking the library catalog and browsing the shelves nearby.

VI. Forms

A form can be a great shortcut in drafting a legal document, especially a document you are drafting for the first time in an unfamiliar area of law. A form provides an excellent starting point by keeping you from reinventing the wheel.

Take care in using any form. Forms are designed for general audiences, not your particular client. Before using a form, ensure that you understand every word in the form and modify it to suit your client's needs. Do not simply fill in the blanks and assume that the form correctly represents your client's position. Unless a particular form is prescribed by statute or by a court, revise the wording to avoid unnecessary legalese.

Forms are available in diverse sources. Oregon statutes provide forms for some particular situations. For example, ORS 107.500 contains forms for a summary procedure for dissolution of marriage. In a non-litigation context, ORS 100.740 contains language that must be included in a condominium sales agreement. To find statutory forms, search the ORS index both for the substantive content of the form and under the term "forms."

Forms may also be found in court rules (discussed in Chapter 5) and CLE materials (discussed in Part V of this chapter). A "form-book" may provide actual forms or suggested language that can be crafted into a form. Examples of Oregon formbooks include *Criminal Law Formbook* and *Advanced Will and Trust Drafting*. Federal forms are available in numerous titles, including *West's Federal Forms* and *American Jurisprudence Legal Forms 2d*. Search the library catalog by subject for topical formbooks.

The Oregon courts have provided a number of litigation-related forms on a website: www.ojd.state.or.us/forms/index.htm. The site has a variety of forms in the areas of tax and family law, as well as forms in other legal areas. The websites of circuit courts may contain additional forms. For example, the Lane County Court link from the site above provides an explanation of and form for obtaining a stalking protective order.

VII. Mini-Libraries and Loose-leaf Services

A "mini-library" combines both primary and secondary sources under one title. In areas of law like taxation and environmental law, a single title may contain statutes, administrative regulations, annotations to cases and agency opinions, and commentary. The benefit is obvious: all of the material is gathered together so that you do not have to consult multiple sources.

A. Print Resources

In print, a topical mini-library is often referred to as a loose-leaf service. This is because the pages are kept in loose-leaf, three-ring notebooks instead of being bound as books. The loose-leaf format allows the publisher to send updates frequently and quickly; the outdated pages are removed and the new pages inserted on a regular basis. A loose-leaf service generally fills numerous volumes. The volumes may be arranged by topic, by statute, or by another system.

Loose-leaf services always have a "How to Use" section, generally near the beginning of the first volume. You should review this section before starting your research. You may also want to skim through a few volumes to become familiar with the organization of that particular service. Pay careful attention to each service's method and frequency of updating.

How you use a loose-leaf service depends on what you know at the beginning of your research. In tax research, for example, if you need to look up a particular section of the Internal Revenue Code (IRC), go to the *Standard Federal Tax Reporter,* and find the volume whose spine indicates that your IRC section is included. Turning to that section, you would find the statutory language, followed by regulations issued by the Treasury Department. Next, you would see annotations to cases decided by courts of general jurisdiction as well as by the United States Tax Court. Also included would be rulings of the Internal Revenue Service. At the end of coverage of that section of the IRC, you would find commentary written by the publisher.

If you do not know the particular section of a loose-leaf that you need to research, begin with the topical index. Often this is the first or last volume of the series. Look up your research terms, and write down the reference numbers given. These will likely be paragraph numbers rather than page numbers. To maintain indexing despite frequent updates, loose-leaf services often are organized by paragraph number. A "paragraph" may be just a few sentences, several actual paragraphs, or many pages in length. Even though the page numbers will change with future updates, the paragraph reference will remain constant.

Turn to each paragraph number referenced in the index under your key terms. Realize that the paragraph number may be for the statute, regulations, annotations, or commentary. Turn to earlier and later pages around that paragraph number to ensure that you have reviewed all relevant material.

B. CD-ROM Services

Recently, "loose-leaf services" are being provided in CD-ROM format. These provide full-text searching in addition to the index searching explained above. For example, Kleinrock Publishing provides the *Standard Federal Tax Reporter* to subscribers monthly in a CD-ROM format called *TaxExpert*.

Using a CD-ROM is fairly straightforward, especially if it simply provides the print material in an electronic format. Look for an index or a search engine to get started in your research. Some CD-ROM products will create a research trail and remember the query words and results; printing these will help you keep track of your research easily.

VIII. Restatements

A restatement is an organized and detailed summary of the common law in a specific legal area. Familiar titles include *Restatement of the Law of Contracts* and *Restatement of the Law of Torts*. Restatements are the results of collaborative efforts by committees of scholars, practitioners, and judges organized by the American Law Institute (ALI). These committees, led by a scholar called the *reporter*, draft text that explains the common law in rule format (*i.e.*, they are written with outline headings similar to statutes, rather than in the narrative form of cases). The committees circulate the drafts for review and revision. The restatement that is published by ALI includes not only the text of the rules that embody the common law but also commentary, illustrations, and notes from the reporter.

Restatements were originally intended simply to restate the law as it existed, in an effort to build national consistency in key common law areas. Over time, restatements grew more aggressive in stating what the authors thought the law should be.

A portion of a restatement becomes primary authority only if it is adopted by a court in a particular case. After a court has adopted a portion of a restatement, the committee's commentary and illustrations, as well as any notes provided by the reporter, may be valuable tools in interpreting the restatement. Cases in other jurisdictions that have adopted the restatement would be persuasive authority.

To find a relevant restatement, search the library catalog for the subject matter or search for "restatement." Within each restatement, use the table of contents, index, or appendix to find pertinent sections. The text of each restatement section is followed by commentary and sometimes illustrations of key points made in the text. Appendix volumes list citations to cases that have referred to the restatement.

Restatements are updated only when a later version is published. Shepardizing a restatement section will reveal cases and articles that cite the restatement.

IX. Uniform Laws and Model Codes

Uniform laws and model codes are written by organizations that hope to harmonize the statutory laws of the fifty states. The most active of these organizations is the National Conference of Commissioners on Uniform State Laws (NCCUSL). Much of the work of writing uniform laws and model codes is done by experts who are law professors, judges, legislators, or attorneys.

Familiar examples of these secondary sources include the *Uniform Commercial Code* (UCC) and the *Model Penal Code*. Statutory language is drafted, then comments are solicited, and the language is finalized. The published uniform law or model code includes both the proposed statutory language and explanatory notes from the authors.

Generally, you would research a uniform law or model code only after one of its provisions had been enacted. At the point a uniform law or model code is adopted by a legislature, it becomes primary authority. The explanatory notes of the uniform law or model rule are very persuasive secondary authority. Reviewing that commentary could help you understand a statute in your jurisdiction that was based on the uniform or model language. For example, every state has adopted a version of the UCC. In researching Oregon's commercial code, you could gain insights from commentary on the UCC that discussed the provisions adopted by Oregon. Additionally, the cases of other states that also adopted the same UCC provisions would be highly persuasive in interpreting Oregon's statute.

Uniform laws and model codes, along with official notes and explanations, are published by the authors. Additionally, commercial versions add commentary and often footnotes with case support. West publishes *Uniform Laws Annotated*, which offers indexing, text, and research annotations to uniform laws prepared under the direction of NCCUSL.

Finding a relevant uniform law or model code is similar to finding a restatement. Search the library catalog for the area of law, such as "criminal law" or "commercial transactions"; you may want to include in your search the words "model code" or "uniform law." In the stacks, scan the titles nearby to determine whether more helpful commercial editions have been published. Within the volume or set of volumes containing the uniform law or model code, look in the table of contents, index, or appendix to locate relevant sections. Often they provide section-by-section indexing of the uniform or model provisions, similar to a digest entry.

X. Ethical Rules

The conduct of lawyers in Oregon is regulated by the Code of Professional Responsibility. The Code consists of Disciplinary Rules (DR) in ten categories, listed in Table 9-5.

The Oregon Code of Professional Responsibility is available in the West deskbook *Oregon Rules of Court: State*. The Code is also available on the Oregon State Bar's website at www.osbar.org/2practice/rulesregs/cpr.htm. Opinions applying these rules to Oregon attorneys are published in *Oregon Formal Ethics Opinions*.

Table 9-5. Code of Professional Responsibility

Disciplinary Rule 1.	Maintaining the Integrity and Competence of the Legal Profession.
Disciplinary Rule 2.	Advertising, Solicitation, and Legal Employment.
Disciplinary Rule 3.	Unlawful Practice of Law.
Disciplinary Rule 4.	Confidences and Secrets of Clients.
Disciplinary Rule 5.	Conflicts of Interest and Mediation.
Disciplinary Rule 6.	Competence and Diligence.
Disciplinary Rule 7.	Zealously Representing Clients Within the Bounds of the Law.
Disciplinary Rule 8.	Improper Conduct as a Public Official or Judicial Candidate; Improper Criticism of the Judiciary.
Disciplinary Rule 9.	Client Funds and Property.
Disciplinary Rule 10.	Definitions.

XI. Jury Instructions

The Oregon State Bar has committees on uniform jury instructions for both civil and criminal matters. Their publications are entitled *Uniform Civil Jury Instructions* and *Uniform Criminal Jury Instructions*. These loose-leaf binders obviously provide uniform instructions for juries in civil and criminal trials; by examining the rules in advance of trial, an attorney may better be able to present evidence to the jury. Even if a case ends before trial, knowing the instructions a jury would receive may produce more effective research.

XII. Using Secondary Sources and Practice Aids in Research

As the above discussions suggest, which source you use will depend on your research project. For a broad overview, an encyclopedia may be best. For in-depth analysis on a narrow topic, an article is more likely to be helpful. On cutting-edge issues, CLE material often covers new areas of law quickly. In litigation, court-approved forms and uniform jury instructions will be indispensable.

Consider your own background in the subject matter and the goals of your research, and select from these sources accordingly. A source that was not helpful in your last research project may be perfect for the current project. How many secondary sources you use depends on the success of your early searches and the time available to you. It would almost never be prudent to check every source discussed in this chapter.

Despite the value of secondary sources, rarely will you cite a secondary source in writing a memorandum or brief. Some sources, such as indexes for finding periodicals, are not "authority" at all. Rather, they are finding tools and should never be cited. Encyclopedias, ALR annotations, and CLE material should be cited only as a last resort. Even sources that are secondary authority, including law review articles and treatises, should be cited infrequently. Instead, cite to primary authority.

Three exceptions exist. First, sometimes you need to summarize the development of the law. If no case has provided that summary, citing a treatise or law review article that traces that development could be helpful to your reader. Citation to secondary authority is also appropriate when there is no law on point for an argument you are making. This is likely to occur with new issues. It may also occur when you are arguing to expand or change the law. In these situations, your only support may come from a law review article. Finally, secondary authority may provide additional support for a point cited to primary authority. For example, you can bolster an argument supported by a case, especially if it is from another jurisdiction, by also citing an article or treatise by a respected expert on the topic.

Whether or not you cite a secondary source in a document, you must decide the weight to give secondary authority in developing your own analysis. Consider the following criteria:

- *Who is the author?* The views of a respected scholar, an acknowledged expert, or a judge carry more weight than a student author or an anonymous editor.

- *When was the material published?* Especially for cutting-edge issues, a more recent article is likely to be more helpful. Even with more traditional issues, be sure that the material analyzes the current state of the law.
- *Where was the material published?* Articles published in established law journals are generally granted the most respect. A school's prestige and the length of the journal's existence influence how well established a journal is. Thus, a journal that has been published for a century at a top law school will carry more respect than a journal at a new, unaccredited school. A publication specific to your jurisdiction or dedicated to a particular topic, however, may be more helpful than a publication from another state or one with a general focus.
- *What depth is provided?* The more focused and thorough the analysis, the more useful the material will be.
- *How relevant is it to your argument?* If the author is arguing your exact point, the material will be more persuasive than if the author's arguments are only tangential to yours.
- *Has this secondary source been cited previously by courts?* If a court has found an article persuasive in the past, it is likely to find it persuasive again. Remember that the text of a secondary source may become primary authority if it is adopted by a court or legislature.

Chapter 10

Online Legal Research

I. Integrating Print and Online Research

Developing a comprehensive research strategy includes deciding when and how to best use online resources.[1] Online resources include commercial providers like LEXIS and Westlaw. Their databases contain enormous numbers of documents and their complex search engines enable the researcher to craft detailed requests. Free online resources maintained by government entities, universities, and law schools provide an increasing number of legal documents. Some of these sites have basic search engines. General search engines like Google and sites with non-legal information may be helpful resources as well.

This chapter reviews some questions you should ask to determine whether to use online sources instead of print sources, outlines some available online resources, and explains how to conduct research online. An appendix at the end of the chapter contains websites for finding Oregon law online.

II. Choosing Print or Online Sources

Online research has a number of advantages. Most significant among these are the ease of searching, the convenience of down-

---

1. While CD-ROMs offer an alternative form of computer researching, they are not discussed in this chapter. The techniques explained here, however, should enable you to use CD-ROMs easily. Realize that CD-ROM products may not be cumulative; updates may be issued monthly on new disks.

loading or printing important documents, and the frequency with which many online sources are updated. Nevertheless, online searching is not always the most effective or cost-efficient way to conduct your research; even fans of online research agree that *beginning* research with books is often more productive than beginning online. Ask yourself the following fundamental questions in deciding whether to use online sources instead of books.

A. *What* is the document?

In print sources, cases, statutes, and commentary often appear in separate books. When looking in a reporter, you know that you are reading a case, not a statute or an article. Cases, statutes, and commentary appear very different from one another in print sources. In contrast, many documents appear the same on a computer screen; for example, a federal statute on a government site and a law student's paraphrased outline of that statute on his personal web page may be shown online in the same font with the same layout.

The difficulty in distinguishing between documents is compounded because hyperlinks in online sources allow you to jump from a case to a statute to an article in a few clicks of a mouse. In an actual library, those moves may take you to different shelves or even different floors. While it is convenient not to leave your computer chair, in reading documents online, you need to pay careful attention to what the document actually is because you can easily lose track of the many different types of sources you click into. As you become a more experienced researcher, you will more quickly be able to distinguish documents online, and the benefits of using print material may likewise decrease.

B. *Who* wrote the document?

Remember that only some documents are binding and authoritative. Documents written by courts, legislatures, and administrative agencies are "the law." Articles and treatises written by recognized experts in a field are not binding, but they can be very persuasive and are often authoritative. Other documents—including law review articles written by students and encyclopedia entries—may be helpful to your research, though they carry less weight. All of these types of documents are available in print and online. Some other documents available online, however, may have been written by a person with little knowledge and may be based only on personal views. Be sure that you know who wrote a document before you base your analysis on it.

Similarly, consider how well the document was edited for accuracy. Print material tends to be more accurate than online material. The very process of publishing ensures a high level of reliability. For a book to appear in a law library, a publisher must first have decided the material in the book had some value. The publisher and author would have edited the document numerous times. Next, a librarian must have decided the book would enhance the collection. The publisher, author, and librarian presumably have reputations to protect through making careful decisions. Because of this careful selection process, print material tends to be more accurate than online versions of the same documents.

In contrast to the time-intensive process of publishing print sources, online material is often valued for the speed with which it becomes available. This means, though, that even reputable services post documents with less editing than a book would warrant. Trusted sources like LEXIS and Westlaw tend to have more typographical errors in their online documents than in their print counterparts. Government websites are also highly reliable, but even those online documents are not "official." Currently, the *print* version of Oregon's laws are considered the official version, even though the state itself maintains a website with those laws available electronically. Aside from well known services and trusted sites, a large body of information is available online, and not all of it is good information. Some of this information may not have been subjected to any quality controls; for a document to appear on a website, a person simply has to know how to post it.

Thus, while there are many excellent online sources for legal authority, you should ask both who wrote the document and how well the document was edited for accuracy.

C. *When* was the material published?

In book research, the copyright date shows when a book's contents were published. In secondary sources, digests, annotated statutes, and other resources, updates are often included in pocket parts or in pamphlets shelved nearby. While it is easy to determine the date of publication and updating of print sources, these sources take longer to reach the researcher than online sources. To find the most current material, online sources often provide a clear advantage. But you still need to determine whether a document has a date indicating when the material was posted or when it was last updated, since some websites may contain outdated material. If a posted or updated date for the document is not available, you should at least note when you visited the website for reference later on.

A related question asks the period of time that an online database covers. Be sure to check every online site or database you use for the scope of coverage, if that information is available. For instance, some online sites may contain materials for only the last few years. Other sites may contain materials from the past twenty years. Finding older material may require using print sources.

Even if you prefer using print sources for other work, you should update sources online with Shepard's or KeyCite rather than a print citator. Updated information is available much more quickly online than in print versions. Also, all the citing sources are listed together in one place, eliminating the need to look at multiple volumes.

D. *How much* context is provided?

Most print sources—and an increasing number of online sources—include tables of contents or outlines that provide an overview of the legal area. For example, a treatise has a table of contents that provides an outline of the book, an encyclopedia includes a topic outline, a digest provides an analysis outline, and a statutory code has a list of statutes under each chapter. These tools can provide context so that a novice researcher can understand the big picture before concentrating on a narrow legal issue.

When searching online, use these tools whenever they are available. Clicking on a table of contents link can show you where your document is placed within related material. This tactic is especially helpful when an online search lands you in the middle of a single document and you lack the visual clues or the context to understand how that document relates to the bigger picture.[2]

Many lawyers—from novices to experts—have stories about the great case or article that they stumbled across in the library stacks while looking for something else. These stories result not just from serendipity, but from being near the area in a resource that puts related information together. Sometimes online searching also produces a serendipitous result; if you feel you may be close but are not finding the exact material you need, try using an online table of contents link to reorient yourself.

E. *How much* does it cost, and who is paying?

Print sources are "free" in the sense that the library has already paid for them. The costs of purchasing and storing print sources continue to rise, and some libraries are finding that online services are less expensive. If you cannot find a source you need in the library, online searching may be your only alternative.

Online sources provided by governments and universities are free. When cost is an issue, consider using these sources first, but do not assume that all commercial sites for computer searches are too expensive. A quick Shepard's search online, with a printout of the results to be found in the stacks, may be much more efficient than hours spent poring over Shepard's volumes that are difficult to read and are not likely up to date. Even other methods of online searching with LEXIS and Westlaw may be relatively inexpensive. Law offices are finding that they can negotiate reasonable flat rates that allow them access to the narrow set of online sources that they use routinely in their practice. This is a great advance from the days when the most

---

2. Westlaw provides a table of contents link to a number of its documents; LEXIS provides a table of contents for statutes and sources like *American Jurisprudence 2d,* a national legal encyclopedia.

significant limitation to online services was the cost. Factors that affected the cost included the number of minutes you were logged on, the number of searches you conducted, and the size of the database or number of sources in which you conducted your searches.

Online searching can still be expensive. A single research project, poorly conceived and sloppily done, could cost hundreds or even thousands of dollars. Be sure that you know the billing practices in your office before making decisions about using online sources that are not free: What is your office's contract with the online provider? How will your office pass along charges to clients? How much are the clients willing to pay? Also, when you do pro bono work, will the firm cover the costs of online searches?

F. *How fast and how efficient* will research be?

Assuming unlimited budgets for both print libraries and online access, many searches could be conducted either in print or online. Depending on your experience and where you are in your research, one form of research may be quicker and more efficient for you than the other. If you have done most of your research in the past in print, you may initially be more comfortable conducting legal research with print sources. Similarly, if you have experience with online searching, you will likely find that online legal research comes to you more easily than it may to some attorneys.

Regardless of your search method, for most researchers a careful reading of search results means using a print version of the document. You can save paper, and sometimes time, by simply taking your list of authorities to *Oregon Reports*, for example, and reading the cases in the books. Take notes as you read. If any case is particularly important, consider copying it. Unless you have negotiated a flat rate for online research that includes printing and downloading, the additional costs for these activities can be prohibitive.

III. Online Sources for Legal Research

A legal researcher can increase the chances of finding accurate material by using highly regarded and dependable sites. The following are examples of established, reputable online research sites. For each site, look for a link such as "Help" or "Searching Hints" to provide information about finding material on that site. Some sites also offer online tutorials to introduce their resources and search processes.

Links to legal research websites referred to in this book will be provided at www.law.uoregon.edu/faculty/srowe/. This list will be updated periodically as web addresses invariably change.

A. Commercial Providers

LEXIS and Westlaw are the largest commercial providers of computerized legal research. Both have reputations for accurate material and user-friendly search techniques. They provide extensive coverage of primary and secondary authority. Other commercial providers of legal materials include Loislaw and VersusLaw. They tend to be less expensive than LEXIS and Westlaw, but they also provide less extensive coverage. Some of these providers allow you to search their sites as a visitor before deciding whether to subscribe to their services.

Table 10-1. Websites for Commercial Providers

Provider	Web Address
LEXIS	www.lexis.com
Loislaw	www.loislaw.com
VersusLaw	www.versuslaw.com
Westlaw	www.westlaw.com

B. Government and University Websites

Government entities and universities often provide access to their website information for free. These sites contain less information than is available from the commercial providers, and the search engines on these sites tend to be more primitive. However, the information available on these sites is increasing, making them more useful research tools. Also, because they are free, they are worth exploring.

Like other states, Oregon maintains its own websites for its primary authority. Although the print versions are the "official" authority, the online versions are useful for research. A chart in the appendix of this chapter contains useful websites for the state constitution, statutes, administrative rules, and judicial opinions. The primary limitation to these sites is that material may be available only for recent years.

In addition, a number of universities maintain websites that provide reliable, though limited information. For Oregon material, the following links are helpful:

- Lewis & Clark Law Library at
  www.lclark.edu/~lawlib
- University of Oregon Law Library at
  http://lawlibrary.uoregon.edu
- Willamette College of Law Library at
  www.willamette.edu/wucl/longlib

Other libraries contain links to valuable sites, even when the library itself does not maintain the material. Two examples are Cornell Law School's Legal Information Institute at www.law.cornell.edu and Washburn University School of Law's "WashLaw" at www.washlaw.edu. The Oregon segments of those websites list links to Oregon cases, statutes, administrative material, and more. A similar "gateway" site is FindLaw at www.findlaw.com.

IV. Searching LEXIS and Westlaw

Each website has a different method for retrieving information, though all tend to follow the same algorithms. Because most websites are constantly being revised and because their search methods change over time, only general information is possible in an overview such as this. The following explanations are primarily for LEXIS and Westlaw,[3] though much of the information should be easily transferable to other online sources.

A. Retrieving a Document When You Have a Citation

When you have a citation to a case, statute, article, or other legal source, retrieving that document online is as simple as typing the citation into a designated box on the proper screen. In LEXIS, click on "Get a Document" and type in the citation. In Westlaw, click on "Find" and type in the citation. Alternatively, each service also allows you to retrieve cases by party name.

B. Continuing Research with "One Good Case"

Once you find an authority that is on point, you can use it as a springboard to find other relevant sources. In LEXIS, you could immediately Shepardize the case to learn of all subsequent cases that cited it. By restricting your Shepard's search to relevant headnotes, you can narrow your search to those subsequent cases that are most likely to be helpful in your research. Alternatively, clicking on a headnote will lead to a Search Advisor screen that allows searching for other cases LEXIS has indexed under the same topic. Other LEXIS options include the "More Like This" or "More Like Selected Text" functions, which ask the computer to find other cases with similar citations or similar language. These are computer-generated searches, however, and the results will be only as good as the program LEXIS has written.

---

3. In addition, LEXIS and Westlaw provide ample training material in print and on their websites. For research assistance, call LEXIS at (800) 455-3947 and Westlaw at (800) 733-2889.

The Westlaw equivalent to Shepardizing is to use the "KeyCite" function. Remember that while Shepard's lists are created by attorneys who read the cases, KeyCite lists are generated by computer. One possible advantage in using Westlaw is the topic-key number system. Once you have a case on point, you can identify the topic-key numbers for relevant headnotes. Then you can use these headnotes as search terms and broaden the list of cases in your results. Clicking on the key number in a case will bring up a screen that prompts a search for additional cases with that key number. Note that in online searching the topic is reduced to a number that precedes a "k" and the key number follows. For example, the topic "Contracts" is assigned the online number 95. Thus, the topic-key number "Contracts 115" on restraint of trade is presented online as 95k115. Topic-key number searching is often most helpful when combined with search terms.

Note that in both LEXIS and Westlaw finding "more" cases does not necessarily mean finding absolutely all other relevant cases. It also does not ensure that the cases retrieved will be relevant. You may find many cases that are not applicable and may detract from your research process. You must analyze the cases yourself and determine whether they are relevant.

C. Researching a Legal Issue from Scratch

Often your work will require you to research issues with no leads and no cites to authorities on point. This section explains the process you should use in these situations. If you are new to online legal searches, your searches may be more successful if you complete the chart in Table 10-2 before beginning your search. Even after you become experienced in online searching, you should still keep notes containing the dates you searched, the searches you ran, and your results from the searches. These notes will help you stay on track while avoiding duplicating research on a later date. Notes will also indicate the time period that needs to be updated as you near your project deadline. Example notes are in Table 10-2.

Table 10-2. Example Notes for Online Searching

Date of Search: *June 20, 2003*

Issue: *Whether a covenant not to compete is enforceable in Oregon*

Online Site or Service: *LEXIS*

Sources: *Oregon state cases (short name: ORCTS)*

Search Terms: *covenant, contract, noncompetition, restraint of trade, compete, employee, employer, employment*

Date Restriction: *Last 10 years*

Search: *(covenant or contract) /p (noncompetition or restraint of trade or compet!) /p employ!*

Results: *[Either list your results here or print a cite list to attach to your notes.]*

1. Clarify the Issue

Searching online does not relieve you of the obligation to carefully think through your legal issue. The computer is no smarter than you are, and it interprets your queries literally. "Garbage in" is likely to result in "garbage out."

2. Choose a Site or Service

First determine where online you will search. Before selecting a commercial service, consider whether the material you hope to find is available from a free, yet reliable, site. As noted earlier, states and universities make a large body of material available that is free and accurate. Sometimes you will have access to just one computer service, for example, if your office subscribes only to Westlaw. If you do have a choice, consider your familiarity with each service, the ease of searching the service, the breadth of resources available through the service, and the cost of the service.

If you select LEXIS or Westlaw, you must also choose which subset of their resources to use. LEXIS and Westlaw divide their vast resources into groups by type of document, topic, and jurisdiction. In LEXIS, these groups used to be called libraries and files, but now they are simply called "sources." In Westlaw, information is grouped into "databases." Each service has a directory to allow you to identify the sources or databases you wish to research. Clicking on the "i" next to the name of the source or database will provide information about its scope.

Try to restrict your search to the smallest set of sources or database that will contain the documents you need. Because online databases correspond to many of the books you have used, it may be helpful to think of yourself in the stacks of the library when choosing sources or databases. Do you really want to search the contents of every reporter on the fourth floor, or do you want to search just Oregon reporters? In addition to producing a more focused set of results, smaller databases also tend to be less expensive than their larger counterparts.

3. Generate Search Terms

Just as in print research, you must generate a list of search terms for online research. Review Chapter 1 for suggestions on generating a comprehensive list of terms.

How you use the terms in online searching is different from how you use them in print research. In print, you look for these terms in indexes and tables of contents to find relevant portions of books. Sometimes this is referred to as "conceptual research" because you are searching indexes for concepts that lawyers have used over time to describe a cause of action, defense, or remedy.

In contrast, in online searching you will most often use these words to search the full text of documents. This is called "full text" searching. There can be disadvantages with this search method. If the author of a particular document does not use the exact term you are searching for, you will not find that document in your results. Not surprisingly, some judges now are careful to write their opinions to include critical terms that will enhance the likelihood that each opinion will be retrieved by researchers in the future.

4. Construct a Search

Both LEXIS and Westlaw, as well as most search engines, allow you to conduct a search simply by typing in a single word. If the word is a term of art like "interpleader" or a cause of action that is less common, for example "kidnapping," this one-word search may be very successful. In contrast, if the search is for a broad area like "murder" or "jurisdiction," you will need to add more terms.

a. Use Boolean Connectors

More comprehensive searches usually result from the use of Boolean[4] connectors. These connectors tell the computer how the terms should be placed in relation to one another in targeted documents, enabling you to more accurately control what the computer searches for. To use Boolean connectors effectively, think of the ideal document you would like to find and try to imagine where your search terms would be located in relationship to each other within that document. Would they be in the same sentence? The same paragraph? Table 10-3 summarizes the most common connectors and commands.

Using the example notes in Table 10-2, searching the terms: *(covenant or contract) /p (noncompetition or restraint of trade or compet!) /p employ!*, the computer will look for:

- either the term *covenant* or *contract*
- within the same paragraph as the term *noncompetition* or *restraint of trade* or variations of *competition, compete, competitor*
- and also in that paragraph variations of *employ, employee, employer, employment.*

Misuse of Boolean connectors can produce bizarre search results. If, instead of "/p" in the example above, the researcher used the "or" connector, the results could include a case in which high school students signed a *covenant* to remain celibate until marriage, a case concerning a *contract* for watermelons, and a case in which a golfer with a disability wanted to *compete* in a tournament without walking between holes.

---

4. George Boole was a British mathematician. The Boolean connectors that carry his name dictate the logical relationship of search terms to each other.

Table 10-3. Boolean Connectors and Commands

Goal	LEXIS	Westlaw
To find alternative terms anywhere in the document	or	or blank space
To find both terms anywhere in the document	and &	and &
To find both terms within a particular distance from each other	/p = in 1 paragraph /s = in 1 sentence /n = within a certain number of words	/p = in 1 paragraph /s = in 1 sentence /n = within a certain number of words
To find terms used as a phrase	leave a blank space between each word of the phrase	put the phrase in quotation marks
To control the hierarchy of searching	parentheses	parentheses
To exclude terms	and not	but not, %
To extend the end of a term	!	!
To hold the place of letters in a term	*	*

b. Online Search Engines

A number of search engines allow you to enter searches without using Boolean connectors. These search engines make their "matches" based on the *location* or the *frequency* of the terms you requested. Location considers where your requested terms appear. The search engine assumes the best matches contain your words in the title, in a heading, or close to the beginning of the site. It may also consider how close together the requested terms are. Frequency-based searching evaluates how often your terms appear; in this case, the search engine assumes that a site that contains your terms more often will be more relevant.

Search engines are designed to show you some results, even if the match does not seem very precise. Sometimes you will review the first ten matches, under the presumption that they are the best, and find that they are irrelevant to your search. This may mean that no better matches exist, that the search was not crafted well enough, or that this particular search engine did not scan the portion of the web that contains the needed documents. Be aware, too, that some matches appear first simply because sponsors pay for this privilege. Sometimes the best match from your perspective was the search engine's fourteenth best match, so skimming through the results is still very important.

c. Natural Language Searching

LEXIS and Westlaw allow natural language searching, which may be most similar to the online searching you have done in the past. You simply type in a question or a list of words and let the computer program decide which words are critical, whether the words should appear in some proximity to one another, and how often they appear in the document.

While natural language searching is unlikely to produce an exhaustive list of relevant authorities, it is likely to result in "one good case" that will spark other research. For this reason, some researchers like to conduct a natural language search early in their research. They skim through the search results quickly to see whether the search netted this one great catch. If so, they use its topic-key numbers or core terms to find other cases, Shepardize or KeyCite it, and search article databases for articles that discuss it.

5. Topic Searching

Both LEXIS and Westlaw allow searching by topic. On LEXIS, the service is called Search Advisor, and it includes two options for searching. Option 1 provides a box for typing in a request. Option 2 provides an extensive outline of the law, beginning with broad categories like Criminal Law, Environmental Law, and Securities Law. Each click narrows the topic of the search.

The West synonym uses topics and key numbers much as you would in an Analysis outline in a digest volume. The KeySearch function shows a list of broad topics like Constitutional Law, Environmental Law, and Intellectual Property. As an example, to research the liability of a corporation to clean up a polluted lake, click on the topic "Environmental Law," then subtopics "Water Pollution" and then "Clean-up Liability." Select the jurisdiction, then the West system will construct a search to find relevant cases. Adding your own terms to the search may help narrow the search to lakes rather than also including ponds, rivers, streams, and other groundwater.

6. Segment and Field Searching

Both LEXIS and Westlaw allow you to search specific parts of documents, such as the date, the author, or the court. The options are available on drop-down menus. In LEXIS these specific parts are called document segments; in Westlaw they are called fields. This type of search is added to the basic search with an appropriate connector.

7. Expanding or Restricting Your Search

Many of your initial searches will locate either no documents or more than 1,000 documents. Do not become frustrated. With practice, you will learn to craft more precise searches that produce more helpful results.

If a search produces no results, use broader connectors (*e.g.*, search for terms in the same paragraph rather than in the same sentence), use more alternative terms, or use a larger set of sources or a larger database. If you still find nothing, consider reading a secondary source to increase your understanding of the issue, researching in print sources, or checking with your supervising attorney.

If your search produces a long list of results, skim them to see whether they are on point. If the results seem irrelevant, modify or edit your search query by omitting broad terms, using more restrictive connectors, or using a smaller set of sources or databases. You can also use the "Focus" feature on LEXIS or the "Locate" feature on Westlaw to narrow your results further. These features allow you to construct a search within a search, and produce a subset of the initial search results. These features may be cost efficient because they do not result in the additional charges of a new search.

Appendix
Where to Find Oregon Law

Links to these sites and others referred to in this book are available online at www.law.uoregon.edu/faculty/srowe.

Oregon Constitution
Print source: *Oregon Revised Statutes*
Government websites:
    www.leg.state.or.us/orcons/home.html
      • contains preamble, text, index, and search engine
    www.leg.state.or.us/billsset.htm
      • contains preamble, text, index, and search engine
LEXIS: ORCODE
Westlaw: OR-ST

Statutes
Print source: *Oregon Revised Statutes*
Government website:
    www.leg.state.or.us/ors
      • provides the index, text of statutes, annotations, rules of civil procedure, and other material from the print version
LEXIS: ORCODE
Westlaw: OR-ST

Agency Rules
Print sources: *Oregon Administrative Rules Compilation* & *Oregon Bulletin*
Government website:
    http://arcweb.sos.state.or.us/banners/rules.htm
      • contains text of *Oregon Administrative Rules Compilation* (OAR) indexed both by the name of the agency and by the OAR chapter number
      • search engine allows searching OAR text
      • site also contains current and past *Oregon Bulletins*
LEXIS: ORREGS
Westlaw: OR-ADC

Judicial Opinions
Print sources: *Oregon Digest; Oregon Reports; Oregon Reports, Court of Appeals;* & *Oregon Tax Reports*
Government website:
    www.ojd.state.or.us
- search engine allows limited, basic searching
- cases are indexed by court and by date of decision
- this site contains slip opinions without editorial enhancements
- only cases from 1998 forward are available

LEXIS: ORCTS
Westlaw: OR-CS

Updating
Print sources: *Shepard's Oregon Citations; Shepard's Pacific Reporter Citations.*
LEXIS: Shepard's
Westlaw: KeyCite

The abbreviations for Westlaw databases and LEXIS sources are available on the scope page, indicated by an "i" next to the database or source name. On Westlaw, the database code can be entered from a box on the directory page. On LEXIS, the short name (also called the file name) can be used in "command searching." In the search box, enter "states," the short name given above, your search query, and .ci (to display a cite list). Separate each by a semicolon. To retrieve a list of Oregon cases on the interplay of ORS 174.020 and the *PGE* case, enter the following search: states;orcts;174.020 & PGE;.ci.

Chapter 11

Research Strategies and Organization

I. Moving from Story to Strategy

In practice, a client will come to your office with a problem and ask for help in solving it. The client will focus on facts that are important to him, without regard to whether they are legally significant. The client may have a desired solution in mind; that solution may best be obtained through legal remedies, or through mediation, family counseling, management strategies, or other means.

Your job will be to sift through the client's story to identify the legal issues. This may include asking questions to probe for facts the client may not immediately remember but which may have important legal consequences. Your job may also include reviewing documents such as contracts, letters, bills, or public records. In addition, you may need to interview other people who are involved in the client's situation.

Sometimes you will not be able to identify the legal issues immediately. Especially in an unfamiliar area of law, you may need to do some initial research to learn about the legal issues that affect the client's situation. Once you have some background in the relevant law, you should determine which legal issues affect the client's situation and begin to formulate a comprehensive research strategy.

II. Planning Your Research Strategy

The research process presented in Chapter 1 contains seven steps: (1) generate a list of *research terms*; (2) consult *secondary sources* and practice aids; (3) find controlling *constitutional provisions*, *statutes*, or *administrative rules*; (4) use *digests* to find citations to cases; (5) read the cases in *reporters*; (6) *update* or "Shepardize" your legal authorities; and (7) *outline* your legal analysis based on your research and *begin writing* your document. After learning how to use each of these resources, you can modify this basic process and design a research strategy that is appropriate for a specific project.

When researching an unfamiliar area of law, you will probably be more successful if you begin with secondary sources. In contrast, if you are familiar with an area of statutory law from previous work, your research may be more effective if you go directly to an annotated code. As a third example, if you are working for another attorney who gives you a citation to a case she knows is relevant, you may want to begin by Shepardizing the case or using its topic-key numbers in a West digest. Both steps may quickly provide more cases on point. Finally, if your supervisor knows that the issue is controlled by common law, you may feel comfortable not researching statutory or constitutional provisions, or spending very little time in those areas.

The research process is not necessarily linear. Research terms are useful in searching the indexes of secondary sources and statutes as well as digests. Secondary sources may cite relevant statutes or cases. Shepardizing may reveal more cases that you need to read, or it may uncover a new law review article that is on point. As you learn more about a project, you may want to review whether your earlier research was effective. Even as you begin writing, you may need to do more research if new issues arise or if you need more support for an argument. The flow chart in Table 11-1 gives an idea of how this process works.[1]

---

1. To simplify an already complicated flow chart, constitutional provisions, administrative law, and legislative history are omitted.

Table 11-1. The Recursive Process of Research

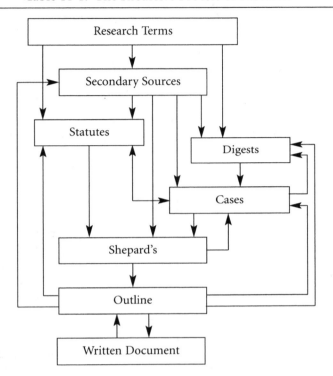

III. Taking Notes

Take careful notes throughout the research process. Taking notes can help you avoid duplicating steps, especially if you have to interrupt your research for a notable length of time. Analytical notes also provide a basis for organizing and writing your document. These notes do not have to be formal or typed; in fact, you might waste valuable time by following too much structure or stopping to type your notes.

Do not underestimate the learning process that occurs while taking notes. Deciding what is important enough to include in notes and expressing those ideas in your own words will increase your understanding of the legal issues involved. Pressing the "print" key and highlighting do not provide this same analytical advantage.

IV. Organizing Your Research

Keeping your research organized is a means to efficient research, not an end in itself. The only "right" way to organize your research is the way that best helps you perform effective research, understand the legal issues, and analyze the problem. The following method will work for taking notes either on a laptop or on a legal pad. For researchers working with paper and pen, "create a document" simply means turning to a new page in your legal pad. Consider using color-coded sticky notes to tab each new document so that you do not get lost in a sea of paper. Some researchers prefer to keep notes of primary authorities on index cards rather than on sheets of paper or in computer files. If so, you will need some sort of box or a combination of clips and rubber bands to keep the cards organized.

Regardless of whether you take notes on your computer or on paper, you will need a three-ring binder or a set of files in which you keep hard copies of the most important authorities. Either tab the binder or label the files with the following headings: strategy/process; secondary sources; list of primary authorities; statutes (include rules and constitutional provisions here); cases; updating; and outline.

Keep organization in perspective. Spending extra time tabbing documents may make you more efficient, or it may be a form of procrastination. Keeping in motion does not necessarily mean making progress; it may just be a form of busy work.

A. Strategy and Process Trail

The first document you create should be your research *strategy*. This is simply a list of the different types of legal resources you intend to search. Writing out your strategy will help you ensure that you check all relevant sources of law. It may also make a new project seem less overwhelming, since the strategy will contain definite steps.

You should refer to this document frequently to be sure you are keeping on track. In developing your strategy, remember to ask yourself the following questions:

- Is this issue controlled by state law, federal law, or both?
- Are there statutes or constitutional provisions on point or is this an area left to common law?
- Are administrative rules or decisions likely to be involved?
- Where in the research process will online sources be more effective and cost efficient than print sources?
- What period of time needs to be researched?
- How long do I have to complete the project?

Feel free to revise your strategy as you learn more about the issues. For instance, you may read a case with a related cause of action that you had not considered or you may encounter an article that highlights a relevant federal claim. If so, you need to adjust your research accordingly.

Your strategy should include a list of research terms that you generate from the facts and issues of your research problem. Brainstorm broadly to develop an expansive list. Refer to this list as you begin work in each new resource. Note on the list which terms were helpful in which resource. Add new terms to the list as you discover them. This list is especially likely to grow during your initial efforts if you begin with a secondary source that provides context for the research project.

Next, begin a *process trail*. While the strategy document outlines what you intend to do in your research, the process trail records what you actually did. By comparing the two, you will stay on track in your research and avoid duplicating work. Some researchers keep copious notes on their strategy document, so that in essence it becomes the process trail. With experience, you will develop a system that is comfortable and efficient for you.

As you begin with a new resource, make notes in your process trail that summarize your work in that resource. For print research, include the volumes you used, the indexes or tables you reviewed, and the terms you searched for. For computer research, include the site, the specific database or link, and the searches that you entered. List both successful and unsuccessful index terms and searches so that you do not inadvertently repeat these same steps later, or so you can revisit a "dead end" that later becomes relevant. Note the date that you performed each search.

Continually look for new authority and use all the resources at your disposal. The following reminders from earlier chapters may help:

- Both the text and footnotes in secondary sources will refer to possibly relevant authority.
- Review pocket parts for recently published information.
- In digests, remember to check both the Descriptive Word Index and the Words and Phrases volumes.
- When you identify a useful topic in a digest, skim its Analysis outline. This will provide an overview of the legal area as well as bring to light new key numbers that might lead to additional cases.
- When reading cases, note earlier cases that are cited. These cases may be highly relevant to your topic.
- With annotated statutes, remember to refer to the library sources that precede the notes of decision. These library sources may reference specific encyclopedia entries, law review articles, or other helpful material.

B. Secondary Authorities

Write a one-page summary for each secondary source you consult. Begin your summary with the title, author, and other citation information for the source. In your own words, summarize the relevant analysis in the source, including references to specific pages. Try to include a few sentences of how this source relates to your research. Does it explain the background of a statute? Does it trace the development of a line of cases? Does it criticize the law in your jurisdiction? Does it suggest a novel approach to your problem? Additionally, note any references to primary authorities that may be on point, and include these in your list of primary authorities.

The goals of reading secondary sources are usually to obtain an overview of an area of law and to locate citations to primary authority. These goals can be met by referring to secondary sources in books in the library or by skimming them online, without the waste of printing out numerous pages of text. Moreover, many law review articles may initially seem helpful but after a few pages they concentrate on a narrow point that is not applicable to your situation.

C. List of Primary Authorities

Create a list of primary sources that will contain the name and citation for all the primary authorities that you need to read. Throughout your research, as you come across a potentially relevant authority, include it on your list. This will allow you to maintain your train of thought with one resource while ensuring that you keep track of important cites to check later. After creating a list that includes a number of sources, check for duplicates before reading the authorities.

D. Analytical Notes on Primary Authority

At frequent points, stop and read the primary authority that you are finding. Legal analysis occurs throughout the process of researching a legal issue; reading as you research will ensure that you are finding relevant material. Note that there are two different modes of reading while you research: fast skimming to determine whether a source is even relevant and slow, methodical reading to understand a relevant authority thoroughly.

Skim each authority first to decide whether it is relevant. This is one of the most time-consuming activities for a novice researcher, but the following suggestions may help. For statutes and rules, skim through sections that provide definitions or explain the purpose. Focus on operative language that sets out duties or proscribes certain conduct. Quickly glance at provisions codified just before or after your provision to see whether they are relevant. For cases, begin by reading the synopsis at the beginning of the case. Then skim the headnotes or core concepts to find the portion of the case that is possibly on point. Go directly to that portion of the case and read it. This probably means skipping over the procedural history, the facts of the case, and analysis of unrelated points of law.

If the source contains relevant material, make a few notes on your list of authorities. If it is not relevant, strike through it on your list. On your computer, use the "reviewing" or "commenting" toolbar to strike through these authorities. Do not completely delete or erase irrelevant authorities; otherwise, you may later find yourself accidentally reading them again.

Once you have selected a number of relevant authorities, choose an organizational scheme for reading them carefully in groups. If there is a constitutional provision, statute, or rule on point, begin by reading it carefully, then move to reading cases that interpret the provision. One approach is to read cases in chronological order, so that you see the development of the law over time. This may be time-consuming for causes of action that have existed for many years. Except for historical research, impose an artificial cut-off of twenty or thirty years in the past, so that you put your effort into recent law. The opposite approach works in many situations: by beginning with the recent cases, you avoid spending time learning old law that has been revised or superseded.

In this second, slower reading of relevant authorities, pay attention to parts that you may have skipped earlier while skimming. Read carefully the definitions in statutes. Be sure you understand the procedural posture of each case, since this affects the standard of review applied. Also be sure that you understand the facts of cases. Drawing a time line or a chart of the relationships between the parties may be helpful. As you read through the case, cross out portions dealing with legal issues that are not confronting your client. If you decide that the case is actually not important, mark that on the first page so that you will not waste time reading it again.

When researching several issues or related claims, consider them one at a time. In this instance, you may have several lists of primary authorities, one for each claim you are researching. You may want to create a different binder or set of folders for each claim.

1. Notes on Statutes

Your notes should include both the actual statutory language and your outline of it. Because the exact words of statutes are so important, you should print, photocopy, or electronically save the text of these provisions.

To fully understand a complex statute, you should outline it. Highlighting is sufficient only if the statute is very short and clear. The statute may provide the elements of the claim or may control the period in which a claim can be brought. Outlining each statute will help you understand it better.

Be sure to refer to the definition sections of statutes; where important terms are not defined, make a note to look for judicial definitions. Also be sure to read statutes that are cross-referenced in any pertinent statute.

2. Notes on Cases

When you decide that a case is relevant, you should brief it. The brief does not have to follow any formal style. Instead, the brief for each case should be a set of notes that highlight the key aspects of the case that are relevant for your research problem. Create a short summary of the pertinent facts, holding, and reasoning. You may choose to do this on your computer, creating a document or a page of a document for each case. You might prefer to write your summary in your legal pad or create an index card. Each case brief should include the following:

- *Citation.* Including the full citation will make writing the document easier because you avoid referring back to the original. Include parallel cites in case the first reporter you check is not later available in your library.
- *Facts.* Include only those facts that are relevant to your project.
- *Holding and reasoning.* Summarize the court's analysis. Again, only address those issues in the case that are relevant to your project. For example, if a case includes both a tort claim and a related contract claim, but the contract claim is not relevant to your project, there is no need for you to thoroughly understand and

take notes on the contract claim. Skim that section to be sure there is no relevant information hidden there, then ignore it.

- *Pinpoint pages.* For case information that you will cite in your written document, include the pinpoint cite. Be sure that the pinpoint is to the authority you have been asked to cite in your document, not a parallel cite. This is especially important when printing online documents in which pagination in different reporters is indicated solely by an asterisk or two.

- *Reflections.* Include your thoughts on the case: How do you anticipate using this case in your analysis? Does it resolve certain issues for your problem? Does it raise new questions?

- *Updating information.* Each case brief should have a designated space for updating. Whether you use Shepard's or KeyCite, you must update each case that you use in your analysis.

E. Updating

You will likely find yourself updating at several points during the research process. Updating with Shepard's or KeyCite early in the process will lead you to other authorities on point. Updating before you begin to rely on an authority is critical; you must verify that each authority you include in your analysis is still "good law." Updating just before submitting a document ensures that nothing has changed while you were working on the project.

Often it is more efficient to update authorities in groups rather than to update each one as you locate it. Take your list of primary authorities to the updating service you plan to use. Update each authority, making notes on your case briefs and statute outlines as to when you updated authorities, whether the authorities are still respected, and what new sources you found. Recording the date of your updating search will be helpful for when you perform your final update just before submitting your document, because you will only have to check citing sources that became available in the interim.

Printing lists of citations is an easy and efficient way to compare new citations with your list of primary authorities. Keep these lists in the *updating* section of your binder.

F. Outlining Your Analysis

Because the most effective research often occurs in conjunction with the analysis of your particular project, try to develop an outline that addresses your client's problem as soon as you can. If outlining feels too restrictive, you may benefit from a chart that organizes all the primary authority by issue or element, such as in Table 11-2, following the typical legal analysis format of Issue-Rule-Application-Conclusion (IRAC).

Your first analytical outline or chart may be based on information in a secondary source, the requirements of a statute, or the elements of a common law claim. It will become more sophisticated and detailed as you conduct your research. Recognize that you cannot reread every case or statute in its entirety each time you need to include it in your outline; instead, refer to your notes and briefs to find the key ideas supporting each step in your analysis.

The outline or chart should enable you to synthesize the law, apply the law to your client's facts, and reach a conclusion on the desired outcome. Applying the law to your client's facts may lead you to research issues that may not be apparent in a merely theoretical discussion of the law.

G. Ending Your Research

One of the most difficult problems new researchers face is deciding when to stop researching and begin writing. Often deadlines imposed by the court or a supervisor will limit the amount of time spent on a research project. The expense to the client will also be a consideration.

Apart from these practical constraints, most legal researchers want to believe that if they search long enough they will find a case or statute or article or *something* that answers the client's legal question clearly and definitively. Sometimes that happens; if you find the answer, you know your research is over. Even without finding a clear answer, when your research in various sources leads back to the same authorities, you can be confident that you have been thorough. As a final checklist, go

Table 11-2. Sample Analysis Chart

<u>Research Question</u>: Can a bent credit card used to break into a store be considered a "burglar tool"?

<u>Controlling Statute</u>: ORS 164.235(2)

Issue	Case	Rule	Application	Conclusion
1. Was the credit card "adapted" to facilitate break-in?	a. *Douglas*	adapted means modified from original design to advance entry; whittled fence post was adapted	card bent but not permanently modified	card probably was not adapted merely by bending it
	b. *Warner*	modification from original purpose must be apparent; signpost used to break into barn was not adapted	modification to card not apparent from examination	
	c. *Reid*	character of thing is more important than specific use; beer bottle used to break into store was not adapted		
2. Was the credit card "designed" to be a burglar tool?	a. *O'Keefe*	burglar tool if used and designed for prying; crowbar is designed, but rock or brick is not	unlike crowbar, card not designed for prying	credit card was not designed to be a burglar tool
	b. *Douglas*	not burglar tool if purpose is different from design; whittled fence post not designed	like fence post, card not designed as burglar tool; purpose is to support a fence/charge items	

through each step of the basic research process to ensure you considered each one. Then review your strategy and process trail for this particular project.

If you have worked through the research process and found nothing, it may be that nothing exists. Before reaching that conclusion, expand your research terms and look in a few more secondary sources. Consider whether other jurisdictions may have helpful persuasive authority.

Remember that the goal of your research is to solve a client's problem. Sometimes the law will not seem to support the solution that your client had in mind. Think creatively to address the client's problem in a different way. While you must tell your supervisor or your client when a desired approach is not feasible, you will want to have prepared an alternate solution if possible.

Appendix A

Legal Citation

To convince another lawyer or a judge that you thoroughly re-searched your argument and that your ideas are well supported, you must provide references to the authorities you used to develop your analysis and reach your conclusion. These references are called *legal citations*. They tell the reader where to find the authorities you rely on and indicate the level of analytical support the authorities provide.[1] In a legal document, every legal rule and every explanation of the law must be cited.

Table A-1. Purposes of Legal Citations

- Show the reader where to find the cited material in the original case, statute, rule, article, or other authority.
- Indicate the weight and persuasiveness of each authority, for example, by specifying the court that decided the case, the author of a document, and the publication date of the authority.
- Convey the type and degree of support the authority offers, for example, by indicating whether the authority supports your point directly or only implicitly.
- Demonstrate that the analysis in your document is the result of careful re-search.

Source: *ALWD Citation Manual.*

---

1. ALWD & Darby Dickerson, *ALWD Citation Manual* 3 (2d ed., Aspen Publishers) ("*ALWD Manual*").

Legal citations are included in the text of legal documents rather than being saved for a bibliography. While you may initially feel that these citations clutter your document, you will soon learn to appreciate the valuable information that they provide.

The format used to convey that information, however, requires meticulous attention to such riveting details as whether a space is needed between two abbreviations. In this respect, citation format rules can be like fundamental writing rules, which are based on convention, not reason. Why capitalize the personal pronoun "I" but not "we" or "you" or "they"? Why does a comma signify a pause, while a period indicates a stop? Rather than trying to understand why citations are formatted the way they are, the most practical approach is simply to learn citation rules and apply them. Frequent repetition will make them second nature.

Of the many different citation systems that exist, this chapter addresses Oregon citation rules as well as the two national citation manuals, the *ALWD Citation Manual: A Professional System of Citation*[2] and *The Bluebook: A Uniform System of Citation*.[3] In law practice, you may encounter state statutes, court rules, and style manuals that dictate the form of citation used before the courts of different states. You may find that each firm or agency that you work for has its own preference for citation or makes minor variations to generally accepted format. Some law offices have their own style manuals, drawn from state rules and national manuals. Once you learn what your employer's preferences are, adjust your citation format to that style. In law school, learn the style of the teacher you are working with or the journal you are a member of. Once you are aware of the basic function and format of citation, adapting to a slightly different set of rules will not be difficult.

---

2. *Id.*

3. *The Bluebook: A Uniform System of Citation* (The Columbia Law Review et al. eds., 17th ed., The Harvard Law Review Assn. 2000).

I. Oregon Citation Rules

Most states have their own rules of citation, called *local rules*. These rules differ somewhat from the rules of other states and the rules in the two national citation manuals. In Oregon, two sources of citation rules are the *Uniform Trial Court Rules* (UTCR) and the *Oregon Appellate Courts' Style Manual* (OSM). Documents filed in Oregon courts must conform to these rules.[4] Lawyers practicing in Oregon generally follow these rules, even when they are not submitting documents to Oregon courts.

Under these rules, no periods are used in reporter abbreviations. Thus, *Oregon Reports* and *Oregon Reports, Court of Appeals* are abbreviated "Or" and "Or App" without punctuation. UTCR 2.010(13); OSM B.1. and B.2. When citing *Oregon Revised Statutes* while working in Oregon, use the abbreviation "ORS." Do not include the date when you are referring to the current code. OSM E.5.

Table A-2. Example Citations Under Oregon Local Rules

Statutes	ORS 164.225.
Cases	*Hoffman v. Freeman Land and Timber, LLC.*, 329 Or 554 (1999). *State v. Reid*, 36 Or App 417 (1978). *Brown v. Bd. of Educ.*, 349 US 294 (1955).
State Rules	OAR 808-003-0010. [Oregon Administrative Rules] ORCP 71 B(1)(b). [Oregon Rules of Civil Procedure]
Federal Rules	FRE 802. [Federal Rules of Evidence]

---

4. For additional Oregon citation rules, see Uniform Trial Court Rule 1.070 and Oregon Tax Court Rule 61. Note, too, that some sources determine how they are to be cited. The preface to *Oregon Revised Statutes* requires that they be cited, for example, as ORS 758.505. Oregon Rule of Civil Procedure 1E states that those rules may be cited according to the following example: ORCP 7 D(3)(a)(i).

190 · Oregon Legal Research

The OSM includes examples of citations for constitutions, legislative material, rules of civil procedure and evidence, administrative rules, and much more. It also contains a writing style guide that addresses such things as capitalization, punctuation, word usage, and parallel construction. If your library does not have a copy of the OSM, you may order one from the Oregon Justice Department's Publications Section at (503) 986-5656.

II. Other States' Citation Rules

If you work in another state, follow that state's local rules or use the format given in the *ALWD Manual* or the *Bluebook*, depending on your supervisor's preferences. In the state of Washington, for example, the Office of Reporter of Decisions publishes a style sheet that determines citations to be used in documents submitted to Washington courts. The abbreviations required by that style sheet are familiar to lawyers practicing in Washington, but may be confusing to lawyers elsewhere.

III. The *ALWD Manual*

While state citation rules often provide just rules and examples, national citation manuals also attempt to explain the components of citations. The *ALWD Manual* is the best manual for novices because it uses a single system of citation for legal memoranda, court documents, law review articles, and all other legal documents. The explanations are clear, and the examples are useful to both law students and practicing attorneys.[5]

---

5. This manual has been adopted by law professors at more than ninety schools. *See* www.alwd.org/cm/ (last visited May 28, 2003). For a helpful review, see M.H. Sam Jacobson, *The ALWD Citation Manual: A Clear Improvement Over the Bluebook*, 3 J. App. Prac. & Process 139 (2001).

A. Citing Oregon Material

Because the *ALWD Manual* is designed for national use, it has different abbreviations for some Oregon material. The most obvious difference is that *Oregon Revised Statutes* is abbreviated "Or. Rev. Stat." instead of "ORS." Since an attorney working in Kansas would not be expected to know whether ORS referred to the statutes of Ohio, Oklahoma, or Oregon, the additional information given by the longer abbreviation is necessary. The *ALWD Manual* also requires reference to the date of the statute, even for the current version.

Another small but important difference is that in the *ALWD Manual* all reporter abbreviations include periods. Thus, the Oregon reporters are abbreviated "Or." for *Oregon Reports* and "Or. App." for *Oregon Reports, Court of Appeals*. Similarly, *Pacific Reporter, Third Series* would be abbreviated "P.3d" rather than "P3d" as under Oregon rules.

A summary of abbreviations for Oregon material appears on page 363 of the *ALWD Manual*.

B. Incorporating Citations into a Document

You must provide a citation for each idea that comes from a case, statute, article, or other source. Thus, paragraphs that state legal rules and explain the law should contain many citations. ALWD 296, Rule 43.2.[6]

A citation may offer support for an entire sentence or for an idea expressed in part of a sentence. If the citation supports the entire sentence, it is placed in a separate *citation sentence* that begins with a capital letter and ends with a period. ALWD 293, Rule 43.1(a). If the citation supports only a portion of the sentence, it is included immediately after the relevant part of that sentence and set off from

---

6. Throughout this chapter, references will be provided to *ALWD* and *Bluebook* pages and rule numbers in this fashion.

Table A-3. Examples of Citation Sentences and Citation Clauses

---

<u>Citation Sentences</u>: First-degree burglary involves a building that is a dwelling. Or. Rev. Stat. § 164.225 (2001). The term dwelling is defined as "a building which regularly or intermittently is occupied by a person lodging therein at night, whether or not a person is actually present." Or. Rev. Stat. § 164.205(2) (2001).

<u>Citation Clauses</u>: Oregon statutes define both first-degree burglary, Or. Rev. Stat. § 164.225 (2001), and second-degree burglary, Or. Rev. Stat. § 164.215 (2001).

---

the sentence by commas in what is called a *citation clause*. ALWD 293, Rule 43.1(b). Table A-3 provides examples of each.

Do not cite your client's facts or your conclusions about a case, statute, or other authority. The following sentence should not be cited: "Under the facts presented, our client's conduct would fall under first-degree burglary, since a homeless family sometimes slept in the building he broke into." These facts and conclusions are unique to your situation and would not be found anywhere in the reference source.

C. Case Citations

A full citation to a case includes (1) the name of the case, (2) the volume and reporter in which the case is published, (3) the first page of the case, (4) the exact page in the case that contains the idea you are citing (*i.e.* the *pinpoint* or *jump* cite), (5) the court that decided the case, and (6) the date the case was decided. ALWD 65–102, Rule 12. The key points in Rule 12 for citation to cases are given below, along with examples.

1. Essential Components of Case Citations

Include the name of just the first party on each side, even if several are listed in the case caption. If the party is an individual, include only the party's last name. If the party is a business or organization, shorten the party's name by using the abbreviations in Appendix 3. ALWD 405–11.

Between the parties' names, place a lower case "v" followed by a period. Do not use a capital "V" or the abbreviation "vs." Place a comma after the second party's name.

The parties' names may be italicized or underlined. Use the style preferred by your supervisor, and use that style consistently throughout each document. ALWD 65, Rule 12.2 (case names); ALWD 13, Rule 1.1 (typeface choice). Do not combine italics and underlining in one cite or within a single document.

EXAMPLE: *Harris v. Fla. Elections Commn.*, 235 F.3d 578, 580
(11th Cir. 2000).

Next, give the volume and the reporter in which the case is found. Pay special attention to whether the reporter is in its first, second, or third series. Abbreviations for common reporters are found on page 76 of the *ALWD Manual.* Oregon reporters are included on page 363. In the example above, 235 is the volume number and F.3d is the reporter abbreviation for *Federal Reporter, Third Series.*

After the reporter name, include both the first page of the case and the pinpoint page containing the idea that you are referencing, separated by a comma and a space. ALWD 33, Rule 5; ALWD 80–81, Rule 12.5. The first page of the above case is 578, and the page where your idea came from is 580. If the pinpoint page you are citing is also the first page of the case, then the same page number will appear twice even though this seems repetitive.[7]

In a parenthetical following this information, indicate the court that decided the case, using abbreviations in Appendix 1 (state courts) and Appendix 4 (federal courts). ALWD 81–83, Rule 12.6. In Appen-

---

7. When using an online version of a case, remember that a reference to a specific reporter page may change in the middle of a computer screen or a printed page. This means that the page number indicated at the top of the screen or printed page may not be the page where the relevant information is located. For example, if the notation *581 appeared in the text before the relevant information, the pinpoint cite would be to page 581, not page 580.

dix 1, the abbreviations for the courts of each state are included in parentheses just after the name of the court. In the above example, the Eleventh Circuit Court of Appeals, a federal court, decided the case.

If the reporter abbreviation clearly indicates which court decided a case, do not repeat this information in the parenthetical. To give two examples, only cases of the United States Supreme Court are reported in *United States Reports*, abbreviated U.S. Only cases decided by the Oregon Court of Appeals are reported in *Oregon Reports, Court of Appeals*, abbreviated Or. App. Repeating court abbreviations in citations to those reporters would be duplicative. By contrast, *Pacific Reporter, Third Series*, abbreviated P.3d, publishes decisions from different courts within several states, so the court that decided a particular case needs to be indicated parenthetically. Thus, in the last example below, "Cal." indicates that the decision came from the California Supreme Court rather than from another court whose decisions are also published in this reporter.

EXAMPLES: *Brown v. Bd. of Educ.*, 349 U.S. 294, 300 (1955).
     Mid-Valley Resources, Inc. v. Engelson, 170 Or. App.
     255, 259 (2000).
     Ketchum v. Moses, 17 P.3d 735, 736 (Cal. 2001).

Note that these court abbreviations are not the same as postal codes. Abbreviating the California Supreme Court as either CA or Calif. would be incorrect.

The final piece of required information in most cites is the date the case was decided. For cases published in reporters, give only the year of decision, not the month or date. Do not confuse the date of decision with the date on which the case was argued or submitted, the date on which a motion for rehearing was denied, or the publication date of the reporter. ALWD 84–85, Rule 12.7.

2. Full and Short Citations to Cases

The first time you mention a case by name, you must immediately give its full citation, including all of the information outlined above. ALWD 53, Rule 11.1; ALWD 441, Appendix 6 (sample memorandum). Even though it is technically correct to include the full citation at the beginning of a sentence, a full citation takes up considerable space. By the time your reader gets through the citation and to your idea at the end of the sentence, the reader may have lost interest.

Table A-4. Examples of Full Citations

Assume that this is the first time the case has been mentioned in this document.

CORRECT:	The intent of the legislature enacting a statute needs to be determined. *Day v. City of Fontana,* 19 P.3d 1196, 1198 (Cal. 2001).
CORRECT: (but should be avoided)	In *Day v. City of Fontana,* 19 P.3d 1196, 1198 (Cal. 2001), the court noted that the intent of the legislature enacting a statute needs to be determined.

After a full citation has been used once to introduce an authority, short citations are subsequently used to cite to this same authority. A short citation provides just enough information to allow the reader to locate the longer citation and find the pinpoint page. ALWD 53–55, Rules 11.2 and 11.3.

When the immediately preceding cite is to the same source and the same page, use *id.* as the short cite. When the second cite is to a different page within the same source, follow the *id.* with "at" and the new pinpoint page number. Capitalize *id.* when it begins a citation sentence, just as the beginning of any sentence is capitalized. ALWD 56.

If the cite is from a source that is not the immediately preceding cite, give the name of one of the parties (generally the first party named in the full cite), the volume, the reporter, and the pinpoint page following "at." ALWD 53–54, Rule 11.2; ALWD 99–100, Rule 12.21(b).

EXAMPLE: Open and notorious possession requires that the claimants prove that the owners had notice that the claimants were asserting title to the disputed property. *Slak v. Porter,* 128 Or. App. 274, 278 (1994). The notice may be actual or constructive. *Id.* at 279. Owners have actual notice when they are aware that their claim of the land is being challenged. *See id.* Constructive notice is satisfied when claimants use the property in a manner considered to give the owner knowledge of their use and claim. *Hoffman v. Freeman Land and Timber, LLC.,* 329 Or. 554, 559 (1999). Construction of a fence is recognized as the classic example of open and notorious possession. *Slak,* 128 Or. App. at 279.

If you refer to the case by name in the sentence, your short citation does not need to repeat the case name, ALWD 100, Rule 12.21(c), though lawyers often do. The last sentence of the example would also be correct as follows: "In *Slak,* construction of a fence was recognized as the classic example of open and notorious possession. 128 Or. App. at 279."

The format, *Slak* at 279, consisting of just a case name and page number, is incorrect. The volume and reporter abbreviation are also needed.

3. Prior and Subsequent History

Sometimes your citation needs to show what happened to your case at an earlier or later stage of litigation. The case you are citing may have reversed an earlier case, as in the example below. If you are citing a case for a court's analysis of one issue and a later court reversed only on the second issue, you need to alert your reader to that reversal. Or, if you decide for historical purposes to include in your document discussion of a case that was later overruled, your reader needs to know that as soon as you introduce the case. Prior and subsequent history can be appended to the full citations discussed above. ALWD 85–90, Rules 12.8–12.10.

EXAMPLE: The only time that the Supreme Court addressed the requirement of motive for an EMTALA claim, the court rejected that requirement. *Roberts v. Galen of Va.,* 525 U.S. 249, 253 (1999), *rev'g,* 111 F.3d 405 (6th Cir. 1997).

D. Federal Statutes

The general rule for citing federal laws is to cite the *United States Code* (U.S.C.), which is the official code for federal statutes. In real-ity, that publication is published so slowly that the current language will most likely be found in a commercial code, either *United States Code Annotated* (published by West) or *United States Code Service* (currently published by LexisNexis). A cite to a federal statute includes the title, code name, section, publisher (except for U.S.C.) and date. The date given in statutory cites is the date of the volume in which the statute is published, not the date the statute was enacted. If the language of a portion of the statute is reprinted in the pocket part, include the dates of both the bound volume and the pocket part. ALWD 108–11, Rule 14.2. If the language appears only in the pocket part, include only the date of the pocket part. ALWD 45, Rule 8.1.

EXAMPLE: (Statutory language appears in both the bound volume and the supplement):
28 U.S.C.A. § 1332 (West 1993 & Supp. 2001).

EXAMPLE: (Statutory language appears in just the supplement):
28 U.S.C.A. § 1332(b) (West Supp. 2001).

E. Signals

A citation must show the reader that you understand the level of support each authority provides. You do this by deciding whether to use an introductory signal and, if so, which one. The more common signals are explained in Table A-5. ALWD 299–302, Rule 44.

F. Explanatory Parentheticals

At the end of a cite, you can append additional information about the authority in parentheses. Sometimes this parenthetical information conveys to the reader the weight of the authority. For example, a case may have been decided *en banc* or *per curiam*. Or the case may have been decided by a narrow split among the judges who heard the case. ALWD 92, Rule 12.11(b). Parenthetical information also allows you to name the judges who joined in a dissenting, concurring, or plurality opinion. ALWD 90–91, Rule 12.11(a). An explanatory parenthetical following a signal can convey helpful, additional informa-

Table A-5. Common Signals

No signal	• The source cited provides direct support for the idea in the sentence. • The cite identifies the source of a quotation.
See	• The source cited offers implicit support for the idea in the sentence. • The source cited offers support in dicta.
See also	• The source cited provides additional support for the idea in the sentence. • The support offered by *see also* is not as strong or direct as authorities preceded by no signal or by the signal *see*.
E.g.	• Many authorities state the idea in the sentence, and you are citing only one as an example; this signal allows you to cite just one source while letting the reader know that many other sources say the same thing.

tion in a compressed space. ALWD 309–11, Rule 46. When using this type of parenthetical, be sure that you do not inadvertently hide a critical part of the court's analysis at the end of a long citation, where a reader is likely to skip over it.

EXAMPLE: Excluding relevant evidence during a sentencing hearing may deny the criminal defendant due process. *Green v. Georgia*, 442 U.S. 95, 97 (1979) (per curiam) (regarding testimony of co-defendant's confession in rape and murder case).

G. Quotations

Quotations should be used only when the reader needs to see the text exactly as it appears in the original authority. Of all the audiences you write for, trial courts will probably be most receptive to longer quotations. For example, quoting the controlling statutory language can be extremely helpful. As another example, if a well known case explains an analytical point in a particularly insightful way, a quotation may be warranted.

Excessive quotation has two drawbacks. First, quotations interrupt the flow of your writing when the style of the quoted language differs from your own. Second, excessive use of quotations may suggest to the reader that you do not fully comprehend the material; it is much easier to cut and paste together a document from pieces of various cases than to synthesize and explain a rule of law. Quotations should not be used simply because you cannot think of another way to express an idea.

When a quotation is needed, the words, punctuation, and capitalization within the quotation marks must appear *exactly* as they are in the original. Treat a quotation as a photocopy of the original text. Any alterations or omissions must be indicated. Include commas and periods inside quotation marks; place other punctuation outside the quotation marks unless it is included in the original text. ALWD 315–31, Rules 47, 48, 49. Also, try to provide smooth transitions between your text and the quoted text.

H. Noteworthy Details

Paying attention to the following details will enhance your reputation as a careful and conscientious lawyer.

- Use proper ordinal abbreviations. The most confusing are 2d for "Second" and 3d for "Third" because they differ from the standard format. ALWD 31–32, Rule 4.3.
- Do not insert a space between abbreviations of single capital letters. For example, there is no space in U.S. Ordinal numbers like 1st, 2d, and 3d are considered single capital letters for purposes of this rule. Thus, there is no space in P.2d or F.3d because 2d and 3d are considered single capital letters. Leave one space between elements of an abbreviation that are not single capital letters. For example, F. Supp. 2d has a space on each side of "Supp." It would be incorrect to write F.Supp.2d. ALWD 17–18, Rule 2.2.
- In citation sentences, abbreviate case names, court names, months, and reporter names. Do not abbreviate these words when they are part of textual sentences; instead, spell them out as in the

example below. ALWD 17–19, Rules 2.1, 2.3; ALWD 405–11, Appendix 3 (months, case names); ALWD 413–15, Appendix 4 (court names); ALWD 374–75, Appendix 1 (federal reporters).

EXAMPLE: The Ninth Circuit held that Oregon's Measure 11 did not violate constitutional rights provided under the Eighth and Fourteenth Amendments. *Alvarado v. Hill,* 252 F.3d 1066, 1069–70 (9th Cir. 2001).

- When *id.* is used to show support for just part of a sentence, this short cite is set off from the sentence by commas and is not capitalized. ALWD 56, Rule 11.3(d).
- It is most common in legal documents to spell out numbers zero through ninety-nine and to use numerals for larger numbers. However, you should always spell out a number that is the first word of a sentence. ALWD 29, Rule 4.2.

IV. The *Bluebook*

Student editors of four Ivy League law reviews have developed citation rules that are published as *The Bluebook: A Uniform System of Citation*, now in its seventeenth edition. An author submitting an article for publication in one of those law reviews, or in other law reviews that adhere to *Bluebook* rules, should follow *Bluebook* citation format. The Oregon Appellate Courts' Style Manual defers to the *Bluebook* for rules not covered in the manual.

Until the *ALWD Manual* was first published in 2000, the *Bluebook* was the only national citation system that was widely recognized. Many law firms, agencies, and organizations still consider *Bluebook* citations the norm, although few practicing lawyers know its current rules; most assume that the *Bluebook* rules have not changed since they were in law school. Section A below explains how to use the *Bluebook* in writing memoranda and briefs. This section points out some areas of change from earlier editions of the *Bluebook* and some differences between the *ALWD Manual* and the *Bluebook* that you may encounter in practice. Section B explains how to use the *Bluebook* in writing articles for scholarly publication.

A. The *Bluebook*: Citations for Practice Documents

For practicing attorneys, the primary difficulty with the *Bluebook* is that it includes *two* citation systems: one for law review articles and another for legal memoranda and court documents. Most of the *Bluebook*'s almost 400 pages are devoted to citations used for articles published in law journals. The rules most important to attorneys, those concerning legal memoranda and court documents, are given about ten pages of attention in the *Bluebook*.

Table A-6. Comparison of *ALWD* and *Bluebook* Formats

ALWD Manual All Documents	*Bluebook* Legal Memoranda	Law Review Articles
Cal. Civ. Proc. Code § 340.5 (West 2001).	Cal. Civ. Proc. Code § 340.5 (West 2001).	CAL. CIV. PROC. CODE § 340.5 (West 2001).

As the example in Table A-6 shows, there is often little or no difference between the final appearance of citations in legal memoranda and court documents using the *Bluebook* and the *ALWD Manual*. However, notice that the *Bluebook* uses a different type—large and small capital letters—for law review citations to the same statute. Because almost all of the *Bluebook* examples are given in law review format, a student or lawyer using the *Bluebook* has to translate each example into the format used in legal documents in practice. The following short guide to the *Bluebook* is included to help you locate pertinent material in the *Bluebook* and translate the examples given there into a useful format for practice documents.

1. Reference Guide and Practitioners' Notes

Perhaps the most helpful information in the *Bluebook* is the reference guide on the inside back cover of the book, which gives examples of citations used in court documents and legal memoranda.[8] Another helpful portion of the *Bluebook* appears on pages 11 through

---

8. Examples of law review citations are found on the inside front cover.

19; these are the Practitioners' Notes. They provide information for and additional examples of citations used in documents other than law review articles. Pages 11 through 13 list items that should be italicized or underlined in citations in legal memoranda and court documents. These include case names, titles of books and articles, and introductory signals. Items not included in the list should appear in regular type. Remember to follow the instructions in this list even when the *Bluebook* examples include large and small capital letters.

2. Index

The index at the back of the *Bluebook* is quite extensive, and in most instances it is more helpful than the table of contents. Most often, you should begin working with the *Bluebook* by referring to the index. Page numbers given in regular type refer to citation instructions, while page numbers in italics refer to examples. Remember that the examples in the body of the *Bluebook* are in law review style. If you are writing a document other than a law review article, you will need to refer also to the practitioners' notes at the front of the book and the examples inside the back cover to see how you must modify the examples.

3. Case Citations

The basic rules for citing cases appear on pages 55 through 73 of the *Bluebook*. The essential material included in case citations is the same under the *Bluebook* and the *ALWD Manual*. The most obvious differences between the two concern abbreviations used in case names. The *Bluebook* lists case name abbreviations in Table T.6, on pages 302 through 303. This list is much shorter than its *ALWD Manual* counterpart. ALWD 407–11. Under the *Bluebook* rule, "United States" is never abbreviated when it is the party's name. BB 62, Rule 10.2.2. Another minor difference between the *Bluebook* and the *ALWD Manual* is the use of apostrophes in abbreviations. The *Bluebook* abbreviates some words with periods and others with apostrophes. The *ALWD Manual* uses only periods. See Table A-7 for some abbreviation comparisons.

The seventeenth edition of the *Bluebook* has changed the rule concerning the abbreviation of the first word of a party's name. Under previous editions, the first word of a party's name could never be abbreviated, unless the name was a common abbreviation like NAACP, the National Association for the Advancement of Colored People. In the current edition, each word in a party's name that appears in T.6 is abbreviated in citations, even if it is the first word.

Table A-7. Comparison of Select Word Abbreviations
in *ALWD* and the *Bluebook*

Word	*ALWD Manual* (Appendix 3)	*Bluebook* (Table T.6)
Associate	Assoc.	Assoc.
Association	Assn.	Ass'n
Center	Ctr.	Ctr.
Commissioner	Commr.	Comm'r
Department	Dept.	Dep't
Hospital	Hosp.	Hosp.

4. Statutes

Citation to statutes is virtually the same under the *Bluebook* and the *ALWD Manual*. Basic statutory citation rules are on pages 76 through 81 of the *Bluebook*.

5. Signals and Parenthetical Information

Introductory signals are covered on pages 22 through 27 of the *Bluebook*. The seventeenth edition of the *Bluebook* changed the rule on the use of the signal *see* back to the rule in force under the fifteenth and earlier editions. The current rule is that *see* is used only to show that the authority offers implicit support for an idea. Under the sixteenth edition, the signal *see* was used before virtually all citations. If you work for attorneys who attended law school while the sixteenth edition of the *Bluebook* was in use (1996–2000), they may not be familiar with the current rule.

The rules for explanatory parentheticals are similar to those in the *ALWD Manual*. Under the *Bluebook* rule, parenthetical information generally should not be given in a complete sentence, but should begin with a present participle (*i.e.*, a verb ending in "-ing") that is not capitalized. BB 28, Rule 1.5.

6. Quotations

There is one slight difference in quotation rules: For the *Bluebook*, quotations that have fifty or more words must be set off in indented blocks. That means the writer must count words to know exactly how many words the quotation contains. BB 43–44, Rule 5.1. In contrast, the *ALWD Manual* requires indented blocks for quotes that are fifty or more words *or* quotes that span four or more lines of typed text. ALWD 318, Rule 47.5.

7. Tables in the Bluebook

Light blue pages at the back of the *Bluebook* contain tables, BB 183–349, with information similar to that given in the *ALWD Manual* appendices, ALWD 333–439. In the first table, however, federal material comes before state material; in the *ALWD Manual* that material comes at end of the first appendix.

8. Differences Between the Bluebook and the ALWD Manual

Comparisons between the *Bluebook* and the *ALWD Manual* are provided in "teaching resources," available at www.alwd.org/cm/.

B. The *Bluebook*: Citations for Law Review Articles

Using the *Bluebook* to write citations for law review articles is considerably easier than using it for practice documents. As noted above, almost all of the examples given in the *Bluebook* are in law review format.

Law review articles place citations in footnotes or endnotes, instead of placing citations in the main text of the document. BB 32, Rule 2.2(a). Most law review footnotes include text in ordinary type,

Table A-8. *Bluebook* **Typeface for Law Review Footnotes**

Item	Type used	Example
Cases	Use ordinary type for case names in full citations. (See text for further explanation.)	Legal Servs. Corp. v. Velazquez, 531 U.S. 533 (2001).
Books	Use large and small capital letters for the author and the title.	DAVID S. ROMANTZ & KATHLEEN ELLIOTT VINSON, LEGAL ANALYSIS: THE FUNDAMENTAL SKILL (1998).
Periodical articles	Use ordinary type for the author's name, italics for the title, and large and small capitals for the periodical.	Robert L. Tsai, *Conceptualizing Constitutional Litigation as Anti-Government Expression: A Speech-Centered Theory of Court Access*, 51 AM. U. L. REV. 835 (2002).
Explanatory phrases	Use italics for all explanatory phrases, such as *aff'g*, *cert. denied, rev'd*, and *overruled by*.	Legal Servs. Corp. v. Velazquez, 531 U.S. 533 (2001), *aff'g* 164 F.3d 757 (2d Cir. 1999).
Introductory signals	Use italics for all introductory signals, such as *see* and *e.g.* when they appear in citations, as opposed to text.	*See id.*

in italics, and in large and small capital letters. This convention is not universal, and each law review selects the typefaces it will use. Some law reviews may use only ordinary type and italics. Others may use just ordinary type. BB 30–32, Rule 2.1.

The typeface used for a case name depends on (1) whether the case appears in the main text of the article or in a footnote and (2) how the case is used. When a case name appears in the main text of the article or in a textual sentence of a footnote, it is italicized. By contrast, if a footnote contains an embedded citation, the case name is written in ordinary text. Similarly, when a full cite is given in a footnote, the case name is written in ordinary type. But when a short cite is used in footnotes, the case name is italicized. Assuming you are submitting an article to a law review that uses all three typefaces, *Bluebook* Rule 2 dictates which typeface to use for each type of authority.

Law review footnotes use short cites generally the same as in other documents. The short cite *id.* can be used only if the preceding footnote contains only one authority. BB 40, Rule 4.1. One unique *Bluebook* requirement is the "rule of five." This rule states that a short cite *id.* can be used if the source is *"readily found in one of the preceding five footnotes."* BB 71, Rule 10.9 (cases) (emphasis in original); BB 89, Rule 12.9 (statutes).

V. Editing Citations

To be sure that the citations in your document correctly reflect your research and support your analysis, you should include enough time in the writing and editing process to check citation accuracy. As you are writing the document, refer frequently to the local rules or to the citation guide required by your supervisor. After you have completely finished writing the text of the document, check the citations carefully again. Be sure that each citation is still accurate after all the writing revisions you have made. For example, moving a sentence might require you to change an *id.* to another form of short cite, or vice versa. In fact, some careful writers do not insert *id.* citations until they are completely finished writing and revising.

Sometimes editing for citations can take as long as editing for writing mechanics. The time invested in citations is well spent if it enables the person reading your document to quickly find the authorities you cite and to understand your analysis.

Appendix B

Selected Bibliography

General Research (tending to focus on federal material)

Robert C. Berring & Elizabeth A. Edinger, *Finding the Law* (11th ed., West 1999).

Morris L. Cohen & Kent C. Olson, *Legal Research in a Nutshell* (8th ed., West 2003).

Christina L. Kunz et al., *The Process of Legal Research* (5th ed., Aspen L. & Bus. 2000).

Roy M. Mersky & Donald J. Dunn, *Fundamentals of Legal Research* (8th ed., Found. Press 2002).

Amy E. Sloan, *Basic Legal Research: Tools and Strategies* (2d ed., Aspen L. & Bus. 2003).

Oregon Research

Karen S. Beck, *Oregon Practice Materials: A Selective Annotated Bibliography*, 88 Law Libr. J. 288 (1996).

Lesley A. Buhman et al., *Bibliography of Law Related Oregon Documents* (AALL 1986).

Specialized Research

Specialized Legal Research (Penny A. Hazelton, ed., 2003 Supp. Aspen L. & Bus.) (formerly edited by Leah F. Chanin).

Ken Kozlowski, *The Internet Guide for the Legal Researcher* (Infosources Publishing 2001).

William A. Raabe, Gerald E. Whittenburg, Debra L. Sanders, John C. Bost, *West's Federal Tax Research* (6th ed., South-Western 2003).

Texts on Legal Analysis

Charles R. Calleros, *Legal Method and Writing* (4th ed., Aspen L. & Bus. 2002).

Linda Holdeman Edwards, *Legal Writing: Process, Analysis, and Organization* (3rd ed., Aspen L. & Bus. 2002).

Linda Holdeman Edwards, *Legal Writing and Analysis* (Aspen L. & Bus. 2003).

Richard K. Neumann, Jr., *Legal Reasoning and Legal Writing: Structure, Strategy, and Style* (4th ed., Aspen L. & Bus. 2001).

Laurel Currie Oates, Anne Enquist, & Kelly Kunsch, *The Legal Writing Handbook: Analysis, Research, and Writing* (3d ed., Aspen L. & Bus. 2002).

Mary Barnard Ray & Barbara J. Cox, *Beyond the Basics: A Text for Advanced Legal Writing* (2d ed., West 2003).

David S. Romantz & Kathleen Elliott Vinson, *Legal Analysis: The Fundamental Skill* (Carolina Academic Press 1998).

Deborah A. Schmedemann & Christina L. Kunz, *Synthesis: Legal Reading, Reasoning, and Writing* (Aspen L. & Bus. 1999).

Helene S. Shapo, Marilyn R. Walter, Elizabeth Fajans, *Writing and Analysis in the Law* (rev. 4th ed., Found. Press 2003).

Index